JOHN MUIR

MODERN SPIRITUAL MASTERS SERIES

JOHN MUIR

Spiritual Writings

Selected with an
Introduction by

TIM FLINDERS

ORBIS BOOKS
Maryknoll, New York 10545

ORBIS BOOKS
Maryknoll, New York 10545

Fathers and Brothers
MARYKNOLL™

Founded in 1970, Orbis Books endeavors to publish works that enlighten the mind, nourish the spirit, and challenge the conscience. The publishing arm of the Maryknoll Fathers and Brothers, Orbis seeks to explore the global dimensions of the Christian faith and mission, to invite dialogue with diverse cultures and religious traditions, and to serve the cause of reconciliation and peace. The books published reflect the views of their authors and do not represent the official position of the Maryknoll Society. To learn more about Maryknoll and Orbis Books, please visit our website at www.maryknollsociety.org.

Library of Congress Cataloging-in-Publication Data
Muir, John, 1838–1914.
    John Muir : spiritual writings / selected with an introduction by Tim Flinders.
       pages   cm. – (Modern spiritual masters series)
    ISBN 978-1-62698-035-8 (pbk.)
    1. Nature—Religious aspects. 2. Muir, John, 1838–1914. 3. Muir, John, 1838–1914—Religion. I. Flinders, Tim. II. Title.
BL65.N35M85 2013
204 – dc23   2013000875

Contents

Sources

DP   *Dear Papa: Letters between John Muir and His Daughter Wanda* (Fresno, Calif.: Panorama West Books, 1985).

JOM   *John of the Mountains: The Unpublished Journals,* ed. Linnie Marsh Wolfe (Madison: University of Wisconsin Press, 1938).

KRS   *Kindred and Related Spirits: The Letters of John Muir and Jeanne C. Carr,* ed. Bonnie Johanna Gisel (Salt Lake City: University of Utah Press, 2001).

LL   *The Life and Letters of John Muir, Vols. 1 and 2,* ed. William Frederic Badè (Boston: Houghton Mifflin, 1924).

MC   *The Mountains of California* (New York: Penguin Classics, 2008)

MFS   *My First Summer in the Sierras* (New York: Random House, Modern Library paperback edition, 2003).

ONP   *Our National Parks* (Boston: Houghton Mifflin, 1917).

ST   *Steep Trails,* ed. William Frederic Badè (Boston: Houghton Mifflin, 1918)

SBY   *The Story of My Boyhood and Youth* (Edinburgh, Scotland: Birlinn Publishers, 2006).

TA   *Travels in Alaska* (New York: Modern Library, 2002).

TMW   *A Thousand-Mile Walk to the Gulf* (Boston: Houghton Mifflin, 1916).

A Timeline of John Muir's Life and Work

1838   April 21, birthday of John Muir, born in Dunbar, Scotland.

1841   Began school at the age of three.

1849   Immigration to Wisconsin at the age of eleven.

1860   Left home to exhibit his inventions at State Agriculture Fair in Madison, Wisconsin.

1861–63 Attends University of Wisconsin for two and a half years, teaches school briefly, forms friendship with his spiritual mentor, Jeanne Carr, wife of university professor Ezra Carr.

1863   Summer, botanical excursion on the Wisconsin River; leaves the university.

1864   March, walks from Wisconsin to Ontario, Canada. Joins brother Dan at Trout Hollow Mill, working eighteen-hour days. Designs machinery to significantly improve the mill's output.

1866   February, Trout Hollow Mill burns down. Muir goes to Indianapolis and finds work in a carriage factory. Finds success as a mechanical engineer.

1867   March, nearly blinded in an accident. Decides to walk to Florida. September–October, walks through the South to Cedar Key, Florida. November, contracts malaria.

1868   January, sails to Cuba, then New York City. March, arrives by ship in San Francisco, walks to Yosemite Valley. April–November, works as a ferryman, sheep shearer, and handyman in Sierra foothills. November, begins work as a shepherd of eighteen hundred sheep in Twenty Hill Hollow, Merced County.

1869   June–September, accompanies two thousand sheep into the high Sierras north of Yosemite Valley. December, moves to Yosemite, builds a cabin at the base of Yosemite Falls and operates a small sawmill.

1870   Works in the sawmill, taking excursions into the high country on Sundays. August, discovers Lyell glacier. December, returns to Twenty Hill Hollow for the winter.

1871   February, returns to Yosemite Valley. May, Ralph Waldo Emerson visits Muir. September, leaves the sawmill and lives on his savings. December, publishes first article on Yosemite glaciers in the *New York Tribune*.

1872   Publishes several articles on Yosemite, builds a cabin on the Merced River. Continues to explore the high country. Spends six weeks in Oakland writing, then races back to Yosemite.

1873   January–October, lives in Oakland. Writes numerous articles. Returns to the Valley in September. November, decides to move permanently to Oakland. His continuous residence in Yosemite ends.

1874–78   Lives with the John Swett family in Oakland. Writes nature articles for the *Overland Monthly* and the *San Francisco Evening Bulletin*. Travels to Nevada, Utah.

1879　　First Alaska trip.

1880　　Marries Louise Strentzel. Second trip to Alaska,
　　　　adventure with Stickeen.

1881　　Manages the Strentzel farm. Birth of Wanda Muir;
　　　　third trip to Alaska.

1882–88　Manages the farm, stops writing and traveling.
　　　　Helen Muir born in 1886. Strentzel family builds a
　　　　mansion in Martinez.

1888　　Trip to Mt. Rainier; editor and contributor of
　　　　Picturesque California, two volumes. Robert Wood
　　　　Johnson persuades Muir to write about a proposed
　　　　Yosemite National Park.

1890　　Muir's Yosemite articles appear in the *Century
　　　　Magazine.* October, Yosemite and Sequoia National
　　　　Parks established by Congress. July, Fourth Alaska
　　　　trip.

1892　　First president of the Sierra Club. Retires from
　　　　farming.

1893　　Trip to Europe. Meets New York literary society,
　　　　revisits his birthplace.

1894　　*The Mountains of California*

1895–98　Publishes two dozen articles and essays in leading
　　　　magazines and newspapers.

1901　　*Our National Parks*

1903　　Accompanies President Theodore Roosevelt to
　　　　Yosemite.

1904　　World tour.

1906　　Yosemite Valley is placed under federal protection.
　　　　Death of Louise Muir, August 6.

Introduction
John Muir's Abiding Light

Not like my taking the veil—no solemn abjuration of the world. I only went out for a walk, and finally concluded to stay out till sundown, for going out, I found, was really going in. —John Muir

The South Tyrolean alpinist Reinhold Messner—climber extraordinaire, first to solo Mt. Everest *without* oxygen—was once asked by an American tourist alarmed at the blight of resorts, spas, and tourist attractions that littered the European Alps, why they had suffered so much more commercialization than the mountains of the American West. "You had Muir," he replied.

Messner did not elaborate, nor did he need to. Most of the Western world knows John Muir as the founder of the environmental movement, the nineteenth-century mountaineer and writer whose articles and political advocacy during the last decades of the nineteenth century galvanized Americans to begin to conserve their rapidly vanishing wilderness. With little more than his pen and an inexhaustible passion for the wild, Muir led the way in reversing the industrialized West's unbridled exploitation of nature. In 1892 Muir helped found the Sierra Club to advance the cause of conservation—the first of its kind—and since that time, millions of acres of America's wetlands and forests, deserts, and high mountains have been set aside for the enjoyment, health, and—decidedly for Muir—the *spiritual* well-being of the American people.

Muir was emphatic about the sacred quality of nature and its restorative effects upon the overly civilized and consequently diminished human spirit. "Get up into the mountains and get close to God," he proclaimed with the fervor of an Old

1

Testament prophet. Yosemite Valley was a *sanctum sanctorum*, the Sierra high country "filled with warm God," a "divine manuscript" as revelatory of the divine as the Bible itself. "Every natural object is a conductor of divinity," he exhorted, "and only by coming into contact with them . . . may we be filled with the Holy Ghost."[1]

Muir wrote from experience. His early journals and letters to his spiritual mentor, Jeanne Carr, describe numerous moments of intimate communion with a "Godful wilderness." Rapt in the glow of an alpine sunset or transported by the unearthly light of a moonlit waterfall where "every bolt and spray feels the hand of God," Muir would frequently slip beyond ordinary physical consciousness into higher states of awareness. "I don't know anything of time, and very little of space," he wrote to Mrs. Carr during his first summer living in Yosemite. "I have spent every Sabbath for the last two months in the spirit world, . . . in unselected atmospheres of terrestrial glory diffused evenly throughout my whole substance."[2]

Immersing himself in the wild was always, for Muir, an essentially spiritual undertaking, a "pilgrimage" to the heart of a sacred natural world. Yet while Muir enjoys a global reputation as the world's preeminent conservationist, far fewer people are aware of his enduring spiritual legacy. Coming of age in a post–Civil War America awash with the promise of material wealth and success, the self-taught, twenty-nine-year-old mechanical engineer resisted the pressures of family, friends, and mentors and, in September 1867, abandoned conventional society to go "wholehearted and unafraid," into the American wilderness. "I bade adieu to mechanical inventions," he wrote about the decisive moment, "determined to devote the rest of my life to the study of the inventions of God."[3] Muir would spend the next several years in an almost unbroken immersion in the mountain wilderness of the central Sierras, often without a blanket and with only tea and flour for food (he did not fish or hunt). It is from out of the crucible of his repeated encounters with the "Divine Soul" he found in the high mountains that Muir would devote himself to proclaiming their restorative powers to the America public. "I care to live only to entice people to look at Nature's loveliness," he wrote to Carr in 1874 when he made the agonizing decision to leave his Yosemite home and enter public life. "Heaven knows that John the Baptist was not more eager to get all his fellow sinners into the Jordan than I to baptize all of mine in the beauty of God's mountains."[4]

The sacred character of Muir's experience in the wilderness is indisputable. Yet its significance to his life and work has often been undervalued or neglected. Preferring to present a more secular and naturalistic Muir to a conventional American audience, his biographers routinely disregarded his more spiritually charged descriptions of nature as Victorian hyperbole. But the primary source of the neglect was Muir himself. From his earliest attempts at journalism in the mid-1870s, he assumed the persona and tone of a nature enthusiast, minimizing or eliminating altogether his more overt spiritual responses to wilderness. Writing in the prevailing literary style of the picturesque, he constructed a romanticized portrait of the Sierra wilderness that would enchant his readers and draw them into the high mountains to "get their good tidings." Intent on advancing his theory of the glacial origins of Yosemite to a skeptical academy, he grounded even his most evocative prose in empirical observation.

But even apart from professional considerations, Muir was temperamentally disinclined to insert his personal experience into his published writing. "My own special self is nothing," he explained to Carr. Writing about his more spiritually charged experiences in the wilderness could prove a distraction or diversion. "As to putting more of myself into these sketches, I am not anxious to tell what I have done," he explained to a Scots cousin who begged him to write more about himself. "It looks too much like having to say, 'Here is the Lord (Nature), and here is Me!' "[5] His most spiritually revelatory work, *My First Summer in the Sierras,* would be published only a few years before his death, while the letters and early journals would not appear until after his passing.[6]

Following the resurgence of interest in Muir that accompanied the rise of the environmental movement in the 1970s, the spiritual dimensions of his life and work have been more readily embraced by biographers. In fact, a consensus appears to be forming that we cannot fully understand Muir or his legacy without accounting for his spirituality.[7]

There are two dimensions to Muir's spiritual legacy that bear special consideration here. First is the modest, but significant body of writing that contains his many lyrical, if not numinous, descriptions of his various encounters with the sacred reality he experienced in the wilderness. There are also the occasional reflections that trace Muir's evolving understanding of creation from biblical orthodoxy to a belief in a more cosmic "law of death and love" that governed life. "All is divine harmony," he exulted from a Georgia cemetery where he had camped for a week in 1867. But his journey to this exalted understanding is littered with conflict and doubt.

In fact, it is this six-year journey of self-discovery that constitutes the second dimension of Muir's spiritual legacy. The story pivots upon two critical moments. The first was his decision in 1867 to abandon professional life, distribute his possessions to friends and family, and enter the American wilderness in an "unconditional surrender" to its call. The second decisive moment occurred six years later when he reluctantly renounced his mountain solitude to settle in the city and, through his writing, persuade Americans to go to the mountains "where everything is wild and beautiful and busy and steeped with God."

Muir's experience of doubt, awakening, "resurrection," and finally acceptance of his calling in the hills and high mountains of the Central Sierras carries echoes of the classical narratives of self-discovery that populate the world's sacred traditions. While the self-effacing Muir would likely chafe at the comparison, his journals and letters to Jeanne Carr trace an archetypal journey of spiritual awakening that can comfortably take its place alongside such American classics as John Woolman's *Journal*, Thoreau's *Walden*, and Thomas Merton's *Seven Story Mountain*.

The spiritual character of Muir's experience in the American wilderness, and especially the many encounters he had there with the sacred, had undeniable effects upon his identity and sense of purpose. It is arguable, in fact, that without these experiences, the John Muir who emerged as the world-historical figure we know today would not have materialized. This will become clearer if we look at Muir's life, and especially at the critical six years of his wilderness pilgrimage.

WISCONSIN, CANADA, INDIANAPOLIS (1838–1867)

Muir was born in Dunbar, Scotland, in 1838 and emigrated with his family to the Wisconsin wilderness in 1849. There he experienced an abusive childhood that included regular beatings from a tyrannical father determined to form him in the image of a stern and unforgiving Calvinism. The young Muir had to forgo his schooling, working the land from before dawn to sunset six days a week. "We were all made slaves to the vice of over-industry," he wrote in his memoirs. "Even when sick we were held to our tasks as long as we could stand."[8] The excessive discipline inured him to the rigors of physical hardship and deprivation, which, ironically, would serve him well in his wilderness solitudes.

Despite the unrelenting demands of a homesteader's life in mid-nineteenth-century America, Muir found endless delight in the wild, verdant Wisconsin wilderness in which he was immersed. He talked to the "bird people" as he ploughed and hoed the fields and came to regard even the flowers and trees as animate beings, an idiosyncrasy he would continue throughout his life. "This sudden flash into pure wildness," he wrote, "how utterly happy it made us." The long immersion in nature appears to have inoculated him against the harsh realities of his youth and allowed his natural exuberance to flourish in spite of them.

Though his formal schooling had ended with his arrival in Wisconsin, Muir became a voracious reader and autodidact. At sixteen, he persuaded his father to let him rise at one each morning so that he could read and study in the cellar before starting out to work at dawn. "I sprang out of bed as if called by a public blast," he wrote of his first morning in the cellar that would quickly become his refuge. He read literature and history, losing himself in Shakespeare, Plutarch, Milton, and the English Romantic poets—fellow Scot Robert Burns, Wordsworth, and Shelley—whose passion for the natural world equaled Muir's and made him realize he was not alone in his worship of nature. He immersed himself in the travels of the European explorers, especially Alexander von Humboldt, the Prussian naturalist whose explorations of the Amazon basin at the beginning of the nineteenth century captivated Muir and planted the idea of his own Amazon exploration.

Muir discovered a technical aptitude as well, teaching himself algebra, geometry, and trigonometry in a single summer. When the cellar was too cold on winter mornings to sit and read, he built a series of ingenious devices that included an early rising bed, a clock that marked the days of the week and month, a self-setting sawmill, and an outdoor thermometer the size of a man.

His was a solitary adolescence. The demanding daily routines left him little time for socializing, while his literary and mechanical obsessions made him appear eccentric to his peers. There is no record of romantic interests. By the time he reached the age of twenty-two, Muir had not ventured beyond a village seven miles from his home. He took over the family farm when his father became an itinerant preacher and seemed destined to live his life in obscurity as a subsistence farmer on the edge of the Wisconsin wilderness.

His talent rescued him. In the summer of 1860, a neighbor suggested he display his inventions at the state fair in Madison, where they created a sensation and attracted the attention of faculty from the University of Wisconsin. Muir attended the university for almost three years, and he was considered likeable, if eccentric, his dorm room full of ingenious time-saving devices that became a point of interest to visitors to the campus. Botany, however, eventually became his ruling passion, and he spent many hours collecting specimens in the forests, bogs, and meadows outside of Madison.

Muir became close with professors who recognized his gifts, including a geologist, Ezra Carr, who introduced Muir to the developing theories of evolution and natural selection—Darwin's *Origin of Species* had been published three years before—notions that challenged his orthodox Calvinist grounding in Genesis. More significantly, Muir came under the tutelage of Jeanne Carr, the professor's wife, a botanist herself from New England who had met Emerson and had been deeply influenced by the transcendentalists. It was a fateful pairing. Carr was the first to recognize Muir's singular genius—she called it the "eye within the eye"—for seeing into the heart of nature. Carr believed that Muir had a calling to carry the transcendentalist vision of a sacred nature to a larger public. It would take years for Muir to accept her assessment, but her support and belief in his promise proved critical. "I have thought of you hundreds of times in my seasons of deepest joy," he wrote her after reaching California in 1868. "Of all my friends, you are the only one that understands my motives and enjoyments."[9] He called her his "spiritual mother."

Muir had arrived in Madison as a pious and dutiful Calvinist, abstemious in his habits and evangelical in his Christian zeal.

He taught Sunday school and visited the army camps—Madison was a recruiting center for the Northern Army—exhorting the young recruits to higher moral standards. Carr introduced Muir to a more liberal Christianity, and he began to move toward a more cosmic, and less biblical, understanding of God and nature. For Carr, and increasingly for the twenty-four-year-old Muir, all nature was divine.

In the summer of 1863, Muir spent several weeks with friends rowing down the Wisconsin River on a botanical excursion that carried him into the heart of the remaining Midwestern wilderness. He left no record of the journey, but his immersion in the wild apparently altered him. Returning to Madison full of "unrest and longing," he dropped out of the university and returned home, with the vague notion of following Von Humboldt's explorations of the Amazon. "I bade my blessed Alma Mater farewell," he concludes the memoir of his youth. "But I was only leaving one University for another, the Wisconsin University for the University of the Wilderness."[10]

Reality, however, intervened. The battle of Gettysburg had claimed fifty-one thousand lives during the weeks Muir was exploring the Wisconsin River, and the Union army was drafting all eligible males into its depleted ranks. Muir, like his mother and brothers, was a pacifist who saw the conflict as a senseless slaughter that had already claimed several of his college friends. With his mother's urging, he decided to join his brother Dan, who had fled to Canada to avoid the war.

In March 1864 Muir set out on foot through the forests of the Great Lakes, sleeping on the open ground, collecting botanical specimens along the way.[11] He reached Ontario in May and found work in a sawmill, where he turned his mechanical talents to improving the mill's output with considerable success. Pressures from his mentors to return to school and his newfound success conflicted him. Still powerfully drawn to wilderness, he nonetheless felt compelled to make a more conventional contribution to society. On an impulse, he applied to the University of Michigan to study medicine and then abruptly changed his mind: "I should like to go to college," he wrote to Jeanne Carr, "but then I have to say to myself, 'You will die ere you can do anything else.' "[12]

In February 1866 the mill was destroyed in a fire, so Muir returned to the United States and found work in a machine factory in Indianapolis, where again his mechanical acumen attracted attention. His wages were doubled after a few months, and his employers offered him the opportunity to become a partner. With introductions from the Carrs, he found his way into Indianapolis society and began to settle into a conventional lifestyle. He taught Sunday school, gave drawing classes to factory workers, and botanized with friends. He saw that his mechanical prowess could bring him wealth and success, a prospect he had not imagined before. The idea of going into the wilderness dimmed and he began to entertain the idea of becoming an inventor. "Now that I am among machines," he wrote to his sister Sarah, "I begin to feel that I have some talent that way, and so I almost think, unless things change soon, I shall turn my whole mind into that channel."[13]

Unless things change . . . On March 15, 1867, a file snapped while Muir was working on a machine and blinded him in the right eye. He was desolate, certain that his intimacy with nature was irretrievably shattered. Carr reassured him. God had given him "the eye within the eye," she counseled, "to see in all natural objects the realized ideas of his mind." Muir was less sanguine. "The sunshine and the winds are working in all the gardens of God," he wrote, "but I—I am lost!"

Muir remained sequestered in a dark room for several weeks while his eye slowly healed. With time to reflect, Muir realized that he had come perilously close to abandoning his dream of exploring the wilderness. He decided to act. "God has to nearly kill us sometimes to teach us lessons," he wrote to

Carr, explaining his decision to turn down the partnership in the machine factory and instead walk a thousand miles to Florida, taking the "leafiest and least-trodden path" he could find. He was not entering the wilderness as "mere sport" or as a "plaything excursion," but "to find the Law that governs the relations subsisting between human beings and Nature."[14] He was well aware of the physical risks that lay ahead of him and acutely sensitive to the displeasure he was leaving behind among his family and mentors. But he felt resigned to a fate he could no longer resist. "I wish I knew where I was going," he wrote Carr. "Doomed to be 'carried of the spirit into the wilderness,' I suppose. I wish I could be more moderate in my desires, but cannot, and so there is no rest."[15]

He called it a "floral pilgrimage," a fusion of field study and sacred journey, encountering the wilderness as both naturalist and pilgrim. In his own mind, he saw something less exalted. "I could have been a millionaire," he wrote many years later, reflecting on his decision: "Instead, I chose to be a tramp." He carried with him a plant press, a botany text, Milton's *Paradise Lost*, a Bible, and a journal to serve both as field log for his botanical observations, and as a record of his personal journey.

THE AMERICAN SOUTH (1867–1868)

Muir's itinerary took him through the deep South, following wagon roads, footpaths, and meandering streambeds through a deeply forested landscape. He describes moods of intense delight as well as darker periods of hunger, fatigue, and melancholy. He was passing through a war-ruined South only two years after the end of the Civil War and often found himself walking through a "warfield" of destroyed crops, shattered farms, and "woods ruthlessly slaughtered." The South was still under the occupation of the Northern army, and Muir, with Wisconsin roots and a Scottish brogue, often met suspicion and even hostility from traumatized southerners.

He reached Savannah, Georgia, in early October and had to wait a few days for funds to arrive that he had left with a brother in Wisconsin. Camping in a large cemetery a few miles from the city, he found himself in a sprawling preserve teeming with great oaks, ancient cypresses, and an almost overwhelming abundance of plants and flowers. The contrast between the funereal statuary that adorned the massive tombs and the profusion of life in the surrounding flowers, plants, and trees evoked a series of epiphanies in which Muir envisioned the natural cycle of birth and death as a "divine harmony." He decried the "morbid death orthodoxy" of his inherited Calvinism, seeing instead only the "beautiful blendings and communions of death and life." Significantly, Muir would find himself near death in a matter of weeks.

He reached Florida in mid-October, disappointed to find an almost impenetrable swampland instead of the flower garden that had for so long stirred his imagination. While he waited for passage to South America, a malarial fever left him unconscious for several days and would have killed him had not a friendly family taken him in and nursed him back to health.[16] In February 1868, "full of malarial poison," he took passage to Cuba, where he spent a month, and then found a ship bound for California. He hoped he could recover his health in the sunshine state and then make his way at last to South America.

THE SIERRAS (1868–1869)

Muir reached California on March 27, 1868, and on an impulse left the next day for Yosemite Valley. Accompanied by a British acquaintance he met aboard ship, Muir walked across the San Joaquin Valley, a five-hundred-mile-long bed of wildflowers. ("Here, here is Florida!" he exulted to Jeanne Carr in a letter.) Muir spent a week in Yosemite and then lived for a year as a shepherd in a remote section of the Sierra foothills known as Twenty Hill Hollow, hoping to one day return to Yosemite on a more permanent basis. One sun-dappled morning in January 1869, Muir found himself transported when "the hollow overflowed with light . . . of an unspeakable richness . . . [and the] . . . sunshine for a whole summer seemed condensed into the chambers of that one glowing day." In what amounts to an initiatory ritual into a sacred world, Muir was carried out of himself: "You lose consciousness of your own separate existence," he wrote of the experience. "You blend with the landscape, and become part and parcel of nature." The epiphany constituted both a "baptism" he said he would never forget and a "resurrection day" after the physical and emotional dark night of the previous months. The solitary, languorous days in the foothills, tending his sheep while immersed in the glowing landscape, restored both his physical health and his spiritual exuberance. "I am well again," he wrote to Carr. "I came to life in the cool winds and crystal waters of the mountains."[17]

In May 1869 Muir seized the opportunity to accompany two thousand sheep into the Sierra high country when he was assured by their owner that he would have ample time to botanize and sketch. Muir spent the summer with the flock in the mountains north of Yosemite Valley "far from the ways and pursuits of man," spending long hours exploring, botanizing, and deciphering the glacial record etched into the Sierra landscape. His journal from these months contains minutely rendered descriptions and sketches of plants, trees, and geological formations, alternating with some of his most inspired and lyrically moving passages. "Oh, these vast, calm, measureless mountain days, inciting at once to work and rest!" he exulted in June. "Days in whose light everything seems equally divine, opening a thousand windows to show us God." A month later, having moved his flock into the meadows of the high country near Tuolumne Meadows, he rhapsodized: "The rocks, the air, everything speaking with audible voice or silent; joyful, wonderful, enchanting, banishing weariness and sense of time. No longing for anything now or hereafter as we go home into the mountains heart. . . . " After reading the manuscript of the journal, his editor at the *Atlantic Monthly* wrote, "I felt almost as if I had found religion."[18]

YOSEMITE (1869–1873)

In December 1869 Muir moved permanently to the Valley. He found work in a small lumber mill and built a cabin at the base of Yosemite falls, channeling a section of the stream to flow beneath his bedroom. He would spend the next four years living in the Valley, using the winter months for reading, journaling, and studying geology. As soon as the snow in the high country retreated, he wandered the peaks and valleys, documenting evidence to support his theory of early glaciation. His approach was novel, blending scientific inquiry with intuitive insight: "This was my method of study," he wrote. "I drifted about from rock to rock, from stream to stream, from grove to grove. Where night found me, there I camped. When I discovered a new plant, I sat down beside it for a minute or day, to make its acquaintance and try to hear what it had to say. . . . I asked the boulders I met, whence they came and whither they were going. . . ."[19]

He became more and more a man of the wild, his hair unkempt, his eyes rapt with an intensity that made him appear to the tourists he met as more Old Testament prophet than naturalist.[20] Beyond caring, Muir luxuriated in his marginalization. "The remnants of compunction," he wrote later about his years in Yosemite, ". . . gradually wasted and melted and at length left me wholly free—born again!"[21]

Friends worried. His siblings regularly urged him to settle down to a conventional life and give up what he himself mocked as his "pathless, lawless thoughts and wanderings." Upon looking at a photograph of his brother from this period, Daniel remarked that he did not recognize Muir's eyes, so intense was their gaze. Jeanne Carr had moved to Oakland in 1869 and pleaded with him to come down from the mountains and take his place in society if he were to fulfill his genius. "You must be social, John," she wrote. "You must make friends among the materialists, lest your highest pleasures, taken selfishly, become impure." While she envied him his mountain solitude, she counseled that "there may be too much of it." Muir resisted: "I have been living in these mountains in so haunting, soaring, floating a way," he offered, "that it seems strange to cast any kind of an anchor. All is so equal in glory, so ocean-like, that to choose one place above another is like drawing dividing lines in the sky."[22] When she persisted, he acknowledged his helplessness: "Although there is no common human reason why I should not see you and civilization in Oakland," he admitted in a letter, "I cannot escape from the powers of the mountains."[23]

Though Muir was always comfortable on his own in the wilderness and luxuriated in extended solo explorations of the back country, he was by no means a recluse. A gifted conversationalist, he enjoyed the company of visitors in Yosemite who shared his love of the mountains. He became close to the Hutchins family, who owned the sawmill, and enjoyed the company of their children. After leaving his job at the mill he guided tourists and began to experience a modest celebrity as the sage of Yosemite.[24] Jeanne Carr sent him regular visitors, including an aging Ralph Waldo Emerson, who visited him in 1871. Emerson found Muir to be an embodiment of the transcendentalist vision, "the right man in the right place," and urged him in a letter to leave his "sequestrations in the solitudes and snows," and join him in the East. "Hurry done with mountains," he implored, "and teach young men in colleges."[25]

Muir would have none of it. "I feel sure that if you were here to see how happy I am, and how ardently I am seeking a knowledge of the rocks," he wrote to Carr after receiving Emerson's summons, "you would not call me away, but would gladly let me go with only God and his written rocks to guide me."[26] But by 1873, Muir was feeling the weight of his social isolation and began to consider a permanent move to the city. He realized that writing could become a vehicle by which he could earn a living, advance his theory of the glacial origins of Yosemite, and proclaim the beauty and spiritual wonder of wilderness. As a trial, he moved temporarily to Oakland in January and wrote a series of articles on the Sierras that appeared in newspapers and magazines both in California and on the East Coast. His article on Sierra glaciation appeared in the *Proceedings of the American Association for the Advancement of Science* at the end of the year, and eventually Muir's theory became widely accepted.

But the months in Oakland proved difficult. The restaurant food did not agree with him, and the "unmixed materialism" of city life grated on his sensibilities. One September afternoon he noticed a goldenrod in bloom along the sidewalk and realized that summer had ended and he had not visited the mountains. Realizing how much he missed the "vital woods and high sky" of the alpine peaks and meadows, he fled to Yosemite, actually running part of the way. "I was wild once more," he wrote, describing his first day back in his Valley home. But something had changed. His effortless, spiritual rapport with the Yosemite landscape eluded him, dimmed by the long immersion in city life. "No one of the rocks seems to call me now," he wrote to Carr shortly after his arrival in Yosemite, "nor any of the distant mountains. "Surely," he concluded, "this Merced and Tuolumne chapter of my life is done."[27]

THE WORLD (1873–1913)

Despite the longing for mountain solitude that would never leave him, Muir moved to Oakland in November 1873 to take up journalism as a career and share with a larger public his enthusiasm for "Godful" nature. When Americans came to love wilderness and to experience its restorative powers, he believed, they would demand its protection. Muir never found writing easy. ("Bookmaking frightens me.") Nor was he entirely sure that there wasn't something "not quite honorable" about the enterprise. Nonetheless, he became a polished and persuasive writer and quickly emerged as a formidable voice for the preservation of wilderness. During the next six years, Muir would publish almost a hundred articles in some of the leading newspapers and journals of the day. He lived in Oakland or San Francisco during the winter months, preparing his articles, and traveled on assignment during the rest of the year among the mountains, deserts, and glaciers of the North American continent, including Alaska. Within a few months of his departure from Yosemite, the solitary life of the thirty-six-year-old mountaineer had blossomed into a demanding routine of travel, speaking, and writing. By the end of the decade, Muir was widely read and sought after as one of the nation's most influential naturalists. But the prolonged, uninterrupted periods of communion with nature had ended.

In 1880, at the age of forty-two, Muir married Louise Strentzel and moved into her father's ranch home in Martinez, California. They had two girls, and for the next eight years he ceased traveling and writing in order to manage the family farm. Muir took only two brief trips to the mountains during that period, and as a consequence his health deteriorated (he had suffered from respiratory problems since his youth). Understanding his need for mountain solitude, his wife urged him to return to the mountains and to his writing. "A ranch that needs and takes the sacrifice of a noble life ought to be flung away beyond all reach and power for harm," she wrote to him in 1888. "The Alaska book and the Yosemite book, dear John, must be written, and you need to be your own self, well and strong, to make them worthy of you."[28]

Muir's most ardent admirers consider his time in Martinez as his "lost" years, since he published nothing during that period and even stopped keeping his journal. But an argument can be made that by domesticating himself as a devoted husband, a loving father, and successful businessman, the onetime wilderness solitary grounded himself in the social and economic conventions of the world that he would one day fundamentally alter. Had he remained sequestered among the "solitudes and snows," it is unlikely that he could have found his place so effortlessly within the corridors of power from which he would recast his vision of a protected, sacred wilderness into public policy.

From a spiritual perspective, Muir's domestic Martinez years, coupled with his agonizing renunciation of his beloved mountains, constitute a recognizable phase in the developmental arc of a prophetic figure. Huston Smith has argued that the stamp of truly exalted spiritual individuals is found not so much in the luminosity of their spiritual intimations of a divine reality, as it is in the character of the life that emerges from the crucible of those experiences. "Even when spiritual experiences are received," Smith writes, "we must distinguish between individuals who experience flashes of insight and others who stabilize these flashes and turn them into abiding light."[29] Viewing the epochal changes that Muir helped enact in American understanding and policy toward wilderness during the two decades following his time as rancher and family man in Martinez, his "lost" years may well be understood more properly as another kind of crucible that enabled him to transmute his many flashes of spiritual insight that marked the Yosemite years into a far more luminous and "abiding light."

The *Century* magazine was the leading literary and intellectual voice of the Eastern establishment in 1888 when its editor, Robert Underwood Johnson, persuaded Muir to join him on a camping trip in the high Sierras. Johnson hoped to induce Congress to create a Yosemite National Park, and he had come west to enlist Muir's support. (Yellowstone had been designated a national park in 1872, but had been left to commercial interests to exploit.) Setting aside large tracts of land free from commercial exploitation was a novel idea, revolutionary even, at a time when most Americans viewed nature as a commodity. During long conversations around a campfire near Tuolumne Meadows, Johnson appealed to Muir to return to journalism—"Has the ink in your fountain dried up?"—and help him make the case for the federal protection of Yosemite.

Johnson proved persuasive. Muir's two articles on Yosemite appeared in the *Century* and provoked an immediate and widespread response among the public.[30] In October 1890 *two* national parks were created, Sequoia and Yosemite (although Yosemite Valley itself remained under the jurisdiction of the state of California). When he heard the news, Muir wrote to Johnson: "That notorious Tuolumne campfire is at last done." Together they had begun to reverse the Western industrial consensus that saw nature as commodity and resource, replacing it with an ethic of conservation that insisted that wilderness preserves were important, "not only as fountains of timber and irrigating rivers, but as fountains of life."[31]

Muir found the work of public advocacy debilitating. His health declined. Against his doctor's orders, he sailed to Alaska in the summer of 1890, claiming that the farther north he traveled, the more his health improved. His brother Daniel moved his family to Martinez in 1891, assuming responsibilities for managing the farm, and Muir found himself financially independent for the first time in his life, "free from the farm and all bread winning cares." In 1892, Robert Johnson, Muir, and others founded the Sierra Club, and Muir agreed to be its president, "to do something for wildness and make the mountains glad."[32] He remained its president until his death in 1913, shaping it into one of the most potent and transformative political forces in American history.

Muir traveled extensively during the decade, and his fame brought him into contact with the leading literary, political, and industrial figures of the day. His first book, *The Mountains of California*, appeared in 1894 and met with far-reaching and immediate success, leading to an upsurge of determination to preserve the nation's forests.[33] Muir's fame grew, as did his income. The abstemious Scot and mountain recluse was now both wealthy and famous, but his highest pleasures still came from mountain wildernesses. As preparation for a book on Yosemite he went alone into the Sierras in 1895 for the first time in two decades. He was fifty-seven. "I will be free in the wilderness again in the old way, without blankets," he crowed to his daughter Wanda in a letter, "but I think I can stand it about as well as ever. The flowers are lovely on the glacier meadows and on the high mountains and you will never know how glad I am to be with them again . . . all the old enthusiasm has come again."[34]

Muir continued to write, partly to argue against attempts by moneyed interests to abolish or restrict the further setting aside of public lands. He continued to travel, returning often to Alaska, since it remained a true wilderness, and eventually he circled the globe. His experience of wilderness, even during his last decades, remained childlike. A sixty-four-year-old Muir is described on one occasion in the high Sierras as throwing up his hands and gesturing to the nearby peaks, "This is the morning of creation! The whole thing is beginning now! The mountains are singing together."[35]

In 1903 Muir accompanied President Theodore Roosevelt (who shared Muir's childlike enthusiasms for the wild) on a three-day camping trip to Yosemite, during which Muir lobbied the president to place the Valley itself under federal protection. Two years later Congress officially appropriated Yosemite Valley as part of the larger Yosemite National Park. "Now that the fight is finished," Muir wrote at the time, "and my education as a politician and a lobbyist is finished, I am almost finished myself."[36]

In August 1905 his wife, Louise, died of cancer, and it would be another six years before Muir would travel again. His daughters had begun families of their own, and he became a doting grandfather. At the urging of many of his friends, Muir finally began to publish the narrative of his life, beginning with *The Story of My Boyhood and Youth* (1910) and *My First Summer in the Sierras* (1911). In acknowledgment of his unique contributions, the largely self-taught Muir received honorary doctorates from Harvard, Columbia, and Berkeley, and in 1912 he realized his lifelong dream of visiting South America. During a newspaper interview in Brazil, Muir remarked that he had no plans to do any more writing until he gave up his current occupation. "And what might that be?" the reporter asked. "Tramp," he replied. "I am seventy-four and still good at it." He died in 1914 from pneumonia.

THEMES

Several spiritual themes are threaded through his early journals and letters, especially those written during his wilderness pilgrimage between 1867 and 1874. These themes can also be located in most of his published nature essays, though usually in a latent form. Among the most prominent are the following:

Sacred Nature

Under the tutelage of Jeanne Carr, Muir came to view the natural world as a revelatory scripture of the Divine. Muir acknowledged that he found more divine inspiration in nature than he found in reading the Bible itself. "Here were miles and miles of tree scripture along the sky," he wrote to Carr in 1874, "a bible that will one day be read. The beauty of its letters and sentences have burned me like fire, through all these Sierra seasons."[37]

For Carr and for Muir, nature's sacred qualities were not readily visible to the undisciplined eye. The "godful wilderness" was revealed only to those who approached nature with reverence, "in a clean condition," having prepared themselves with an ascetic rigor. "Only in this way can we procure our daily spirit bread," Muir insisted. A natural ascetic, Muir was famous for his ability to spend days and weeks in the high wilderness with little more than flour, to bake bread, and tea. "Just bread and water in delightful toil is all I need," he crowed during his first summer in the mountains: "not unreasonably much, yet one ought to be trained and tempered to enjoy life in these brave wilds in full, independent of any particular kind of nourishment."[38]

With his inherited Calvinist background Muir is not likely to have been conversant with traditional Catholic contemplative traditions, yet he seems to have intuited the practice of prayer and fasting as a means of gaining intimations of "divine wildness." In a letter to his sister Sarah from above Yosemite, he mentioned that he had time each day to sketch, to write, and to "meditate." He once climbed to a ledge next to Yosemite Falls to "spend the night in prayer," and on another, he camped for several days amid the giant Sequoias south of Yosemite, "fasting and praying for light." A few months later, having climbed to a ledge above his cabin in Yosemite in the predawn, Muir witnessed the continuing revelation of nature's "Great Soul" as the sun rose over the Valley walls: "The trees, the mountains are not near or far; they are made one, unseparate, unclothed, open to the divine soul, dissolved in the mysterious incomparable spirit of holy light! . . . They seem to wait only in the very special presence of the great soul!"[39]

Cosmic Unity

Underlying Muir's vision of the world is the recognition of a divine continuity that streams through the cosmos, joining humans in their fundamental nature with the flora and fauna of the natural world. "Wonderful, how completely everything in wild nature fits into us, as if truly part and parent of us," he exclaimed during his first week in the Sierra wilderness. "The sun shines not on us but in us. . . . The trees wave and the flowers bloom in our bodies as well as our souls."[40]

His reflections on this deeper unity range from intimate discourses with plants, such as his encounter with a calypso orchid in the Canadian wilderness—"It seemed the most spiritual of all the flower people I had ever met. I sat down beside it and fairly cried for joy"—to sweeping declarations of a cosmic unity that anticipated both modern cosmology and the theological speculations of Christian theologians like Pierre Teilhard de Chardin and Father Thomas Berry. "The whole wilderness seems to be alive and familiar, full of humanity," he wrote of the Sierras in 1869. "The very stones seem talkative, sympathetic, brotherly. No wonder when we consider that we all have the same father and mother."[41]

While living in Yosemite, Muir received a letter from an Indianapolis mentor who was critical of his decision to remain in the wilderness, apart from his fellow men and women. "You say that good men are 'nearer to the heart of God than are woods and fields, rocks and waters,'"Muir responded with uncharacteristic heat. "Rocks and waters, etc., are words of God and so are men. We all flow from one fountain Soul. All are expressions of one Love."[42]

Equality

During his difficult trek through the cypress swamps of Florida in 1867, Muir was dismayed and sometimes frightened by the exotic and unfamiliar animal life he encountered there. In time, though, he sensed a kinship with all the wild creatures, and began to question the biblical account of creation that placed "Lord Man" above them. Muir argued that every being had been created for itself, rather than to serve "Lord Man." His reflections on this theme during his thousand-mile walk include some of his most emphatic and acerbic prose. "How narrow we, selfish, conceited creatures are in our sympathies!" he declared from his perch in a Florida swamp—"how blind to the rights of all the rest of creation!"

Muir also rejected the Calvinist insistence upon a "fallen" nature that was inherently evil. "Though alligators, snakes, etc., naturally repel us," he wrote, "they are not mysterious evils. They dwell happily in these flowery wilds, are part of God's family, unfallen, undepraved, and cared for with the same species of tenderness and love as is bestowed on angels in heaven or saints on earth." He ends these speculations with a defense of the alligator, which more than once had frightened him during his trek through Florida. "May you long enjoy your lilies and rushes," he declares in full sympathy with this maligned creature, "and be blessed now and then with a mouthful of terror-stricken man by way of dainty!"[43]

Some years later, in Alaska, Muir continued his criticism of orthodox religious attitudes towards the animal world. "See the narrow selfishness of the attitude of man in dealing with animals, selfish even in religion," he wrote, after his instructive adventure with the "child-dog" Stickeen: "for after stretching to the utmost his mean charity, he admits every vertical mammal, white, black, or brown, to his heaven, but shuts it against all the rest of his fellow mortals. Indian dogs go to the happy hunting grounds with their masters—are not shut out."[44]

Muir continued to expand these insights and came to believe that all nature was graced with the Divine. "We speak of higher forms, higher types," he argued in his journal in 1873, but "all of the individual 'things' or 'beings' into which the world is wrought are sparks of the Divine Soul variously clothed upon with flesh, leaves, or that harder tissue called rock."[45]

An Indwelling Spirit

Muir's break with his inherited Calvinism is no more evident than in his sense of an indwelling divine presence that animates a natural world "where everything is wild and beautiful and busy and steeped with God." Far from the transcendent God of Genesis that commands nature from above, Muir's "warm God" inhabits the universe and fills it with light and harmony. It was a "blessed thing to go free in the light of this beautiful world," Muir wrote to a friend, "to see God playing upon everything, as a man would play on an instrument."[46]

Muir was not a pantheist. Nowhere does he imply that nature is God. Rather, all the varied forms of nature "are simply portions of God ... made terrestrial by the clothes they wear and by the modifications of a corresponding kind in the God essence itself."[47] This presence is most palpably felt in the "cold mountain altitudes," where "Spirit is but thinly and plainly clothed."

The Creation Cycle

Following his epiphanies in the Bonaventure cemetery near Savannah in 1867, Muir renounced his biblical understanding of death as distinct from life or as entry to a more exalted state of being. He saw life and death functioning naturally as a unity, a "harmony of love and death," and proclaimed that, for him, immersion in this natural cycle would be immortality enough. Later, in the Sierras, the cycle of life, death, and regeneration became more strikingly visible to Muir, who now saw that nothing in nature was wasted. "It is eternally flowing from use to use, beauty to yet higher beauty," he wrote during his first summer in the mountains, "and we soon cease to lament waste and death ... and faithfully watch and wait the reappearance of everything that melts and fades and dies about us."[48]

Near the end of his life, Muir was certain of the eternal flow of the cosmic cycle in which all of nature participated, including himself. "All the merry dwellers of the trees and streams . . . go home through death," he wrote in a journal fragment during his final year, "all alike passed on and away under the law of death and love. Yet all are our brothers and they enjoy life as we do, share heaven's blessings with us, die and are buried in hallowed ground, come with us out of eternity and return into eternity."[49]

THE SELECTIONS

Since the majority of Muir's spiritual writings are found among his journals and letters, I have organized these selections chronologically, beginning in 1864 with his stay in Canada. Selections include his frequent rapturous descriptions of "divine wildness" in its many forms, as well as early passages that express his many doubts and conflicts about his destiny, including his struggles to balance the claims of the world against those of the spirit.

1

The Eye within the Eye
Canada, Indiana (1864–1867)

In March 1864 Muir left his Wisconsin home and walked to Canada, where he lived and worked in a small broom-making mill in Trout Hollow near Meaford, Ontario. He worked eighteen-hour days, designing and building machinery that tripled the number of broom handles produced by the mill, while at night he studied botany, sleeping only a few hours.

The following selection is excerpted from Muir's first letter to Jeanne Carr, his spiritual mentor, and it begins a correspondence that will continue, albeit sporadically, until her passing in 1903. Muir's letters to Carr from this period reveal an earnest, disciplined, but struggling twenty-seven-year old, conflicted by competing desires to contribute to society as an inventor or physician, or to go into the wilderness and study "the inventions of God." His Wisconsin professors encouraged him to study medicine, and one sent him a letter of recommendation, which apparently was lost en poste.

Trout Hollow, Ontario, September 13, 1865
Letter to Jeanne Carr

Your precious letter with its burden of cheer and good wishes has come to our hollow, and has done for me the work of sympathy and encouragement which I know you kindly wished it to do. It came at a time when much-needed, for I am subject to lonesomeness at times.

I am sorry over the loss of Prof. Sterling's letter, for I waited and wearied for it a long time. I've been keeping up in the regular course of study since leaving Madison, but with no great success. I do not believe that study, especially of the natural sciences, is incompatible with ordinary attention to business; still, I seem to be able to do but one thing at a time. Since undertaking a month or two ago to invent new machinery for our mill, my mind seems to so bury itself in the work that I am fit for little else; and a lifetime is so little a time that we die ere we get ready to live. I would like to go to college, but then I have to say to myself, "you will die ere you can do anything else." I should like to invent useful machinery, but it comes, "you do not wish to spend your lifetime among machines and you will die ere you can do anything else." I should like to study medicine that I might do my part in helping human misery, but again it comes, "you will die ere you are ready or able to do so."

How intensely I desire to be a Humboldt! [and explore the wilderness]. . . .

I was struck with your remarks about our real home of stillness and peace. How little does the outer and noisy world in general know of that "real home" and real inner life! Happy indeed they who have a friend to whom they can unmask the workings of their real life, sure of sympathy and forbearance!

You propose, Mrs. Carr, an exchange of thoughts, for which I thank you very sincerely. This will be a means of pleasure and improvement which I could not have hoped ever to have been possessed, but then here is the difficulty: I feel that I am altogether incapable of properly conducting a correspondence with one so much above me. We are, indeed, as you say, students, in the same life school, but in very different classes. I am but an alpha novice in those sciences [of Nature] which you have studied and loved so long.   —KRS, 29–31

Trout Hollow, Ontario, January 21, 1866
Letter to Jeanne Carr

Dear Mrs. Carr,

Your last, written in the delicious quiet of the Sabbath in the country, has been received and read a good many times. I was interested with the description you draw of your sermon. You speak of such services like one who appreciated and relished them. But although the page of Nature is so replete with divine truth, it is silent concerning the fall of man and the wonders of Redeeming Love. Might she not have been made to speak as clearly and eloquently of these things as she now does of the character and attributes of God? It may be a bad symptom, but I will confess that I take more intense delight from reading the power and goodness of God from "the things which are made," than from the Bible. The two books, however, harmonize beautifully and contain enough of divine truth for the study of all eternity. Oh it is so much easier for us to employ our faculties upon these beautiful tangible forms [in nature], and to exercise a simple, humble, living faith such as you so well described. . . .

I have been very busy of late making practical machinery. I like my work exceedingly well . . . I sometimes feel as though I was losing time here but I am at least receiving my first lessons in practical mechanics. . . . The school is a pretty good one.

—KRS, 34–36

The following letter to Carr was written in Canada sometime between October 12 and December 16, 1866. It contains the earliest expression we have of the rapturous epiphanies Muir experienced in the wilderness and vividly illustrates their power to raise him above physical consciousness. [50]

Date Unknown, 1866?
Letter to Jeanne Carr

The rarest and most beautiful of the flowering plants I discovered on this first grand excursion was *Calypso borealis* (the Hider of

the North). I had been fording streams more and more difficult
to cross and wading bogs and swamps that seemed more and
more extensive and more difficult to force one's way through.
Entering one of these great tamarac and arbor-vitae swamps one
morning, holding a general though very crooked course by compass, struggling through tangled drooping branches and over
and under broad heaps of fallen trees, I began to fear that I
would not be able to reach dry ground before dark. . . .

But when the sun was getting low and everything seemed
most bewildering and discouraging, I found beautiful Calypso
on the mossy bank of a stream, growing not in the ground but
on a bed of yellow mosses in which its small white bulb had
found a soft nest and from which its one leaf and one flower
sprung. The flower was white and made the impression of the
utmost simple purity like a snowflower. No other bloom was
near it, for the bog a short distance below the surface was still
frozen, and the water was ice cold. It seemed the most spiritual
of all the flower people I had ever met. I sat down beside it and
fairly cried for joy.

It seems wonderful that so frail and lowly a plant has such
power over human hearts. . . . How long I sat beside Calypso I
don't know. Hunger and weariness vanished, and only after the
sun was low in the west I plashed on through the swamp, strong
and exhilarated as if never more to feel any mortal care.

—LL, 1:120–22

*In February 1866, the Trouts' mill burned down, so Muir
returned to the United States and settled in Indianapolis, finding
work in a wheel factory where his mechanical talents quickly
established him as a promising young industrialist. On March 6,
1867, an iron filing broke away, piercing the edge of his right cornea and nearly blinding him. After a month-long sequestration
in a darkened room, his eyesight recovered, and Muir decided to
embark on a thousand-mile walk to Florida. From there, following Von Humboldt, he planned to sail to the Amazon.*

Indianapolis, May 7, 1866
Letter to Daniel Muir

I have about made up my mind that it is impossible for me to escape from mechanics. I begin to see and feel that I really have some talent for invention, and I just think that I will turn all my attention that way at once. . . . I mean now, Dan, to give my whole attention to machines because I *must*. . . . I cannot get my mind upon anything else.[51]

Indianapolis, May 1866
Letter to Sarah Muir Galloway

I *feel* something within, some restless fires that urge me on in a way very different from my *real* wishes, and I suppose that I am doomed to live in some of these noisy commercial centers.

Circumstances over which I have had no control almost compel me to abandon the profession of my choice [explorer] and to take up the business of an inventor, and now that I am among machines I begin to *feel* that I have some talent that way, and so I almost think, unless things change soon, I shall turn my whole mind into that channel.[52]

Indianapolis, April 3, 1867
Letter to Jeanne Carr

Dear friend, you have of course heard of my calamity. The sunshine in the winds are working in all the gardens of God, but I—I am lost.

I am shut in darkness. My hard, toil-tempered muscles have disappeared, and I am feeble and tremulous. . . .

My friends here are kind beyond what I can tell and do much to shorten my immense blank days. I send no apology for so doleful a note because I feel, Mrs. Carr, that you will appreciate my feelings. —KRS, 44

Indianapolis, April 6, 1867
Letter to Jeanne Carr

Your precious letter of the 15th reached me last night. I am much better than when I [last] wrote you; can now sit up about all day and in a room partly lighted. . . .

The eye is pierced just where the cornea meets the sclerotic coating. I do not know the depth of the wound or its exact direction. Sight was completely gone from the injured eye for the first few days, and my physician said it would be ever gone, but I was surprised to find that on the fourth or fifth day I could see a little with it. Sight continued to increase for a few days, but for the last three weeks it has not perceptibly increased or diminished. . . .

When I received my blow, I could not feel any pain or faintness because the tremendous thought glared full on me that my *right eye* was lost. I could gladly have died on the spot, because I did not feel that I could have heart to look at any flower again. But this is not so, for I wish to try some cloudy day to walk to the woods, where I am sure some of spring's sweet fresh-born are waiting.

I believe with you that "nothing is without meaning and purpose that comes from a father's hand," but during these dark weeks I could not feel this, and, as for courage and fortitude, scarce the shadows of these virtues were left me. The shock upon my nervous system made me weak in mind as a child. But enough of woe. . . .

I thank you all again for your kindness. I cannot make sentences that will tell how much I feel indebted to you. . . .

—KRS, 44–46

Indianapolis, August 30, 1867
Letter to Jeanne Carr

We are safely in Indianapolis. I am not going to write a letter, I only want to thank you and the Doctor and all of the boys for the enjoyments of the pleasant botanical week we spent with you. . . .

I wish I knew where I was going. Doomed to be "carried of the spirit into the wilderness," I suppose. I wish I could be more moderate in my desires, but cannot, and so there is no rest. Is not your experience the same as this?

I feel myself deeply indebted to you all for your great and varied kindness—not any the less if from stupidity and sleepiness I forgot on leaving to express it.   —KRS 57

2

Floral Pilgrimage
The American South (1867–1868)

On September 1, 1867, Muir crossed the Ohio River from Indiana into Kentucky and set out on a thousand-mile "floral pilgrimage" to Florida, taking the "wildest, leafiest," and "least trodden" route he could find. Tying a blank journal to his waist, often scribbling or sketching in the dim light of a campfire, he recorded his observations on the flowers, trees, animals, and people he encountered along the way. Despite his complaints about the difficulties of the writing process, his journals often reflect a fluid, engaging prose.

The following passage describing his departure appears in autobiographical notes found among his papers.

As soon as I got out into heaven's light [after the accident], I started on another long excursion, making haste with all my heart to store my mind with the Lord's beauty, and thus be ready for any fate, light or dark. And it was from this time that my long, continuous wanderings may be said to have fairly commenced. I bade adieu to mechanical inventions, determined to devote the rest of my life to the study of the inventions of God. . . . When they asked where I was going. I said, "Oh! I don't know—just anywhere in the wilderness, southward. . . . And if possible to wander far enough into South America to see tropical vegetation in all its palmy glory."[53]

Inscription on the flyleaf of the journal:

John Muir. Earth. Planet. Universe.

Kentucky, September 1, 1867

Few bodies are inhabited by so satisfied a soul as to allow exemption from extraordinary exertion through a whole life. The sea, the sky, the rivers have their ebbs and floods, and the earth itself throbs and pulses from calms to earthquakes. So also there are tides and floods in the affairs of men, which in some are slight and may be kept within bounds. But in others it is constant and cumulative in action until its power is sufficient to overmaster all impediments, and to accomplish the full measure of its demand. For many a year I have been impelled toward the Lord's tropic gardens of the South. Many influences have intended to blunt or bury this constant longing, but it has outlived and overpowered them all. They overmaster everything.[54]

Kentucky, September 2, 1867

I had long been looking from the wild woods and gardens of the Northern States to those of the warm South, and at last, all draw-backs overcome, I set forth [from Indianapolis by train] on the first day of September, 1867, joyful and free, on a thousand-mile walk to the Gulf of Mexico. Crossing the Ohio at Louisville [September 2], I steered through the big city by compass without speaking a word to anyone. Beyond the city I found a road running southward, and after passing a scatterment of suburban cabins and cottages I reached the green woods and spread out my pocket map to rough-hew a plan for my journey.

My plan was simply to push on in a general southward direction by the wildest, leafiest, and least trodden way I could find, promising the greatest extent of virgin forest. Folding my map, I shouldered my little bag and plant press and strode away among the old Kentucky oaks, rejoicing in splendid visions of pines and palms and tropic flowers in glorious array, not, however,

without a few cold shadows of loneliness, although the great
oaks seemed to spread their arms in welcome.   —TMW, 1–2

Kentucky, September 8, 1867

Deep, green, bossy sea of waving, flowing hilltops. Corn and
cotton and tobacco fields scattered here and there. . . . The scenery on approaching the Cumberland River becomes still grander.
Burkesville, in beautiful location, is embosomed in a glorious
array of verdant flowing hills. The Cumberland must be a happy
stream. I think I could enjoy traveling with it in the midst of such
beauty all my life. This evening I could find none willing to take
me in, and so lay down on a hillside and fell asleep muttering
praises to the happy abounding beauty of Kentucky.

—TMW, 13–14

Tennessee, September 10, 1867

Toward the top of the Cumberland grade, about two hours
before sundown. . . . Arriving at the last house, my knock at the
door was answered by a bright, good-natured, good-looking little woman, who in reply to my request for a night's lodging and
food, said, "Oh, I guess so. I think you can stay. Come in and
meet my husband. . . ."

When he came in after his hard day's work and sat down to
dinner, he solemnly asked a blessing on the frugal meal, consist-
ing solely of corn bread and bacon. Then, looking across the
table at me, he said, "Young man, what are you doing down
here?" I replied that I was looking at plants. "Plants? What
kind of plants?" I said, "Oh, all kinds; grass, weeds, flowers,
trees, mosses, ferns—almost everything that grows is interesting
to me."

"Well, young man," he queried, "you mean to say that you are
not employed by the Government on some private business?"
"No," I said, "I am not employed by anyone except just myself. I
love all kinds of plants, and I came down here to these Southern

States to get acquainted with as many of them as possible." "You look like a strong-minded man," he replied, "and surely you are able to do something better than wander over the country and look at weeds and blossoms. These are hard times, and real work is required of every man that is able. Picking up blossoms doesn't seem to be a man's work at all in any kind of times."

To this I replied, "You are a believer in the Bible, are you not?" "Oh, yes." "... Do you not remember that Christ told his disciples to 'consider the lilies how they grow,' and compared their beauty with Solomon in all his glory? Now, whose advice am I to take, yours or Christ's? Christ says, 'Consider the lilies.' You say, 'Don't consider them. It isn't worthwhile for any strong-minded man.'"

This evidently satisfied him, and he acknowledged that he had never thought of blossoms in that way before. He repeated again and again that I must be a very strong-minded man, and admitted that no doubt I was fully justified in picking up blossoms. He then told me that although the war was over, walking across the Cumberland Mountains still was far from safe on account of small bands of guerrillas who were in hiding along the roads, and earnestly entreated me to turn back and not to think of walking so far as the Gulf of Mexico until the country became quiet and orderly once more.

I replied that I had no fear, that I had but very little to lose, and that nobody was likely to think it worth while to rob me; that, anyhow, I always had good luck. In the morning he repeated the warning and entreated me to turn back, which never for a moment interfered with my resolution to pursue my glorious walk.   —TMW, 20–26

Tennessee, September 12, 1867

Crossed a wide cool stream [the Emory River], a branch of the Clinch River. There is nothing more eloquent in nature than a mountain stream, and this is the first I ever saw. Its banks are luxuriously peopled with rare and lovely flowers and overarching trees, making one of nature's coolest and most hospitable places. Every tree, every flower, every ripple and eddy of this lovely stream seemed solemnly to feel the presence of the great creator. Lingered in this sanctuary a long time thanking the Lord with all my heart for his goodness and allowing me to enter and enjoy it. —TMW, 30

Tennessee, September 18, 1867

Up the mountain on the state line. The scenery is far grander than any I ever before beheld. The view extends from the Cumberland mountains on the North, Florida, Georgia and North Carolina to the South, an area of about 5,000 miles. Such an ocean of wood, waving, swelling mountain beauty and grandeur is not to be described. . . . Oh, these forest gardens of our father! What perfection, what divinity, in their architecture! What simplicity and mysterious complexity of detail! —TMW, 38–39

The following entries were written while Muir was spending a week in the Bonaventure cemetery on the outskirts of Savannah, Georgia, waiting for money to arrive that he had left with his brother. The contrasts between the funereal atmosphere of the cemetery with the teeming "light and life" of the natural setting, induced a series of reflections upon life and death which, for some biographers, amount to a conversion experience. These signal Muir's break from the biblical account of creation in Genesis towards a more universal understanding that places humans within an eternally renewing natural cycle of life, death, and regeneration.

Savannah, Georgia, October 9, 1867

After going again to the express office and post office, and wandering about the streets, I found a road which led me to the Bonaventure graveyard. If that burying-ground across the

Sea of Galilee, mentioned in Scripture, was half as beautiful as Bonaventure, I do not wonder that a man should dwell among the tombs. . . .

The most conspicuous glory of Bonaventure is its noble avenue of live oaks. They are the most magnificent planted trees I have ever seen. . . . Large flocks of butterflies, all kinds of happy insects, seem to be in a perfect fever of joy and supportive gladness. The whole place seems like a center of life. The dead do not reign there alone.

Bonaventure to me is one of the most impressive assemblages of animal and plant creatures I ever met. I was fresh from the western prairies, the garden-like openings of Wisconsin . . . but never since I was allowed to walk the woods have I found so impressive a company of trees as the tillandsia-draped oaks of Bonaventure.

I gazed awe-stricken as one new-arrived from another world. Bonaventure is called a graveyard, a town of the dead, but the few graves are powerless in such a depth of life. The rippling of living waters, the song of birds, the joyous confidence of flowers, the calm, undisturbable grandeur of the oaks, mark this place of graves as one of the Lord's most favored abodes of life and light.

On no subject are our ideas more warped and pitiable than on death. Instead of the sympathy, the friendly union, of life and death so apparent in nature, we are taught that death is an accident, a deplorable punishment for the oldest sin, the archenemy of life, etc. Town children, especially, are steeped in this death orthodoxy, for the natural beauties of death are seldom seen or taught in towns.

But let children walk with nature, let them see the beautiful blendings and communions of death and life, their joyous inseparable unity, as taught in woods and meadows, plains and mountains and streams of our blessed star, and they will learn that death is stingless indeed, and as beautiful as life, and that the grave has no victory, for it never fights. All is divine harmony.
—TMW, 66–71

Savannah, Georgia, October 10, 1867

The traces of war are not only apparent on the broken fields, burnt fences, mills, and woods ruthlessly slaughtered, but also on the countenances of the people. A few years after a forest has been burned another generation of bright and happy trees arises, in purest, freshest vigor; only the old trees, wholly or half dead, bear marks of the calamity. So with the people of this warfield. Happy, unscarred, and unclouded youth is growing up around the aged, half-consumed, and fallen parents, who bear in sad measure the ineffaceable marks of the farthest-reaching and most infernal of all civilized calamities. . . . Yet I still press eagerly on to Florida as the special home of the tropical plants I am looking for, and I feel sure I shall not be disappointed.

—TMW, 84, 85

Upon arriving in Florida, Muir was indeed disappointed not to find the "bright blooming vines" and floods of bright sunlight he had dreamed about, but instead salt marshes, and "vine-tied" swamps which made the pathless wanderings he favored difficult, if not impossible to follow. A meditation on his kinship with the alligator underscores the distance he has traveled from Calvinist orthodoxy.

Florida, October 15, 1867

Today, at last, I reached Florida, the so-called "Land of Flowers," that I had so long waited for, wondering if after all my longings and prayers would be in vain and I should die without a glimpse of the flowery Canaan. . . . In visiting Florida in dreams, of either day or night, I always came suddenly on a close forest of trees, every one in flower, and bent down and entangled to network by luxuriant, bright-blooming vines, and overall a flood of bright sunlight. But such was not the gate by which I entered the promised land. Salt marshes, belonging more to sea than to the land; with groves here and there, green, and unflowered, sunk to the shoulders in sedges and rushes. . . .

Everything in earth and sky had an impression of strangeness; not a mark of friendly recognition, not a breath, not a
spirit whisper of sympathy came from anything about me, and
of course I was lonely. I lay on my elbow eating my bread, gazing, and listening to the profound strangeness.

While thus engaged I was startled from these gatherings of
melancholy by a rustling sound in the rushes behind me. Had
my mind been in health and my body not starved, I should
only have turned calmly to the noise. But in this half-starved,
unfriended condition, I could have no healthy thoughts, and I at
once believed that the sound came from an alligator. I fancied I
could feel the stroke of his long notched tail, and could see his
big jaws and rows of teeth, closing with a springy snap on me,
as I had seen in pictures.

Well, I don't know the exact measure of my fright, either in
time or pain, but when I did come to a knowledge of the truth,
my man-eating alligator became a tall white crane, handsome
as a minister from spirit land—"only that." I was ashamed and
tried to excuse myself on account of Bonaventure anxiety and
hunger.

Florida is so watery and vine-tied that pathless wanderings
are not easily possible in any direction. . . . I was meeting so
many strange plants that I was much excited, making many
stops to get specimens. But I could not force my way far through
the swampy forest, although so tempting and full of promise.
Regardless of water snakes or insects, I endeavored repeatedly
to force a way through the tough vine tangles, but seldom succeeded in getting farther than a few hundred yards. . . .

It was while feeling sad to think that I was only walking on
the edge of the vast wood that I caught sight of the first Palmetto
in a grassy place, standing almost alone. A few magnolias were
near it, and bald cypresses, but it was not shaded by them. They
tell us that plants are perishable, soulless creatures, that only
man is immortal, etc.; but this, I think, is something that we

know very nearly nothing about. Anyhow, this palm was indescribably impressive and told me grander things than I ever got
from human priest. . . .

I am now in the hot gardens of the Sun, where the palm meets
the pine, longed and prayed for and often visited in dreams, and,
though lonely tonight amid this multitude of strangers, strange
plants, strange winds blowing gently, whispering, cooing, in
a language I never learned, and strange birds also, everything
solid or spiritual full of influences that I never before felt, yet I
thank the Lord with all my heart for his goodness in granting me
admission to this magnificent realm.   —TMW, 87–93

Florida, October 16, 1867

Last evening when I was in the trackless woods, the great mysterious night becoming more mysterious in the thickening darkness, I gave up hope of finding food or a house bed, and searched
only for a dry spot on which to sleep safely hidden. . . . But even
the sandy barren was wet, and I had to grope in the dark a long
time, feeling the ground with my hands when my feet ceased to
plash, before I at last discovered a little hillock dry enough to lie
down on. I ate a piece of bread that I fortunately had in my bag,
and drank some of the brown water about my precious hillock,
and lay down. . . .

Another man that I met today pointed to a shallow, grassy
pond before his door. "There," said he, "I once had a tough fight
with an alligator. He got my dog. I heard him howling, and as he
was one of my best hunters, I try hard to save him. . . ."

I never in all my travels saw more than one [alligator], though
they are said to be abundant in most of the swamps, and frequently attain a length of nine or ten feet. It is reported, also,
that they are very savage, oftentimes attacking man. . . .

Many good people believe that alligators were created by the
devil, thus accounting for their all-consuming appetite and ugli-
ness. But doubtless these creatures are happy and feel the place

assigned them by the great creator of us all. Fierce and cruel they appear to us, but beautiful in the eyes of God. They, also, are his children, for he hears their cries, cares for them tenderly, and provides their daily bread.

The antipathies existing in the Lord's great animal family must be wisely planned, like balanced repulsion and attraction in the mineral kingdom. How narrow we, selfish, conceited creatures are in our sympathies! how blind to the rights of all the rest of creation! With what dismal irreverence we speak of our fellow mortals! Though alligators, snakes, etc., naturally repel us, they are not mysterious evils. They dwell happily in these flowery wilds, are part of God's family, unfallen, undepraved, and cared for with the same species of tenderness and love as is bestowed on angels in heaven or saints on earth.

I think that most of the antipathies which haunt and terrify us are morbid productions of ignorance and weakness. I have better thoughts of those alligators now that I have seen them at home. Honorable representatives of the great saurians of an older creation, may you long enjoy your lilies and rushes, and be blessed now and then with a mouthful of terror-stricken man by way of dainty!   —TMW, 93—99

In October, Muir was stricken with a severe bout of malaria that almost proved fatal. He spent November and December recuperating in Cedar Key, Florida, and then in January 1868 sailed to Cuba where he stayed for a month. He continues his reflections on creation, emphatically challenging (and mocking) his inherited Calvinist orthodoxy.

Cedar Key, Florida, October 23, 1867

The very day after reaching the sea I began to be weighted down by inexorable leaden numbness which I resisted and tried to shake off for three days, by bathing in the Gulf . . . I did not fear any serious illness, for I never was sick before and was unwilling to pay attention to my feelings.

But yet heavier and more remorselessly pressed the growing fever, rapidly gaining on my strength . . . about the middle of the afternoon, the fever broke on me like a storm, and before I had staggered halfway to the mill (to work) I fell down unconscious on the narrow trail among dwarf palmettos. . . .

How long I lay unconscious I never found out, but it must have been many days. Some time or other I was moved on a horse from the mill quarters to Mr. Hodgson's house [his employer] where I was nursed about three months with unfailing kindness, and to the skill and care of Mr. and Mrs. Hodgson I doubtless owe my life. [Despite] quinine and calomel—in sorry abundance—with other milder medicines, my malarial fever became typhoid. I had night sweats, and my legs became like posts of the temper and consistency of clay on account of dropsy. So on until January, a weary time. . . .

During my long sojourn here as a convalescent I used to lie on my back for whole days beneath the ample arms of these great trees, listening to the winds and the birds. . . .

The world, we are told, was made especially for man—a presumption not supported by all the facts. A numerous class of men are painfully astonished whenever they find anything, living or dead, in all God's universe, which they cannot eat or render in some way what they call useful to themselves. They have precise dogmatic insight on the intentions of the creator. . . . He is regarded as a civilized, law-abiding gentlemen in favor either of a republican form of government or of a limited monarchy; believes in the literature and language of England; is a warm supporter of the English Constitution and Sunday schools and missionary societies; it is as purely a manufactured article as any puppet of a half-penny theater.

With such views of the creator, it is of course not surprising that erroneous views should be entertained of the creation. To such properly trimmed people, the sheep, for example, is an easy problem—food and clothing, "for us," eating grass and daisies white by divine appointment for this predestined purpose, on perceiving the demand for wool that would be occasioned by the eating of the apple in the garden of Eden. . . .

Now, it never seems to occur to these farseeing teachers that nature's object in making animals and plants might possibly be first of all the happiness of each one of them, not the creation of all for the happiness of one. Why should man value himself as more than a small part of the one great unit of creation? And what creature of all that the Lord has taken the pains to make is not essential to the completeness of that unit—the cosmos? The universe would be incomplete without man; but it would also be incomplete without the smallest trans-microscopic creature that dwells beyond our conceitful eyes and knowledge.

From the dust of the earth, from the common elementary fund, the creator has made *Homo sapiens*. From the same material, He has made every other creature, however noxious and insignificant to us. They are earth-born companions and our fellow mortals. . . . This star, our own good Earth, made many a successful journey around the heavens ere man was made, and whole kingdoms of creatures enjoyed existence and returned to dust ere man appeared to claim them. After human beings have also played their part in creation's plan, they too may disappear without any general burning or extraordinary commotion whatever. . . .

But, glad to leave these ecclesiastical fires and blunders, I joyfully return to the immortal truth and immortal beauty of Nature.   —TMW, 127–42

Muir's ship encountered a tropical storm during its passage to Cuba. Against the advice of the captain, Muir tied himself above decks to observe the storm.

The Gulf of Mexico, January 1868

"You had better go below," said the captain. "The Gulf Stream, opposed by this wind, is raising a heavy sea and you will be sick. No Landsman can stand this long." I replied that I hoped the storm would be as violent as the ship could bear, that I enjoyed the scenery of such a sea so much that it was impossible to be sick, that I had long waited in the woods for just such a storm, and that now that the precious thing had come, I would remain on deck and enjoy it.

"Well," said he, "if you can stand this, you are the first Landsman I ever saw that could."

I remained on deck, holding on by a rope to keep from being washed overboard, and watched the behavior of the *Belle* as she dared nobly on; but my attention was mostly directed among the glorious fields of foam-topped waves. The wind had a mysterious voice and carried nothing now of the songs of birds, or of the rustling of palms and fragrant vines. Its burden was gathered from a stormy expanse of crested waves and briny tangles. I could see no striving in those magnificent wave motions, no raging; all the storm was apparently inspired with nature's beauty and harmony. Every wave was obedient and harmonious as the smoothest ripple of a forest lake, and after dark all the water was phosphorescent like silver fire, a glorious sight.

—TMW, 145–46

Havana, Cuba, January 16, 1868

The daily programme for nearly all the month that I spent here was about as follows: After breakfast a sailor rowed me ashore on the north side of the harbor. A few minutes' walk took me past the Morro Castle and out of sight of the town on a broad cactus common, about as solitary and untrodden as the tangles of Florida. Here I zigzagged and gathered prizes among unnumbered plants and shells along the shore, stopping to press the plant specimens and to rest in the shade of vine-heaps and bushes

until sundown. The happy hours stole away until I had to return
to the schooner. . . . The [Havana] strand, as far as I walked it,
was luxuriously fringed with woody Compositae, two or three
feet in height, their tops purple and gold and with a profusion
of flowers. Among these I discovered a small bush whose yellow
flowers were ideal; all the parts were present, regularly alternate,
and in fives, and all separate, a plain harmony. . . .

There is not a fragment in all nature, for every relative fragment of one thing is a full harmonious unit itself. All together
form the one grand palimpsest of the world.

—TMW, 151–64

3

Baptism and Resurrection
The Sierras (1868–1869)

Muir arrived in San Francisco aboard ship on March 27, 1868, and immediately left for Yosemite Valley, where he spent a week. He then hired on as a shepherd in a remote, uninhabited area called Twenty Hill Hollow in the Sierra foothills. An educated, thirty-year-old without prospects, he began to question the choices that found him living in a "gray box" of a hermit's shack overseeing eighteen hundred sheep, far from civilized life. But the wild, profuse beauty of the Sierra landscape restored his health and altered him irretrievably. The months in Twenty Hill Hollow and the powerful unitary visions he experienced there, continued the "conversion" process begun at Bonaventure.

Twenty Hill Hollow, July 26, 1868
Letter to Jeanne Carr

I have had the pleasure of but one letter since leaving home from you. That I received at Gainesville, Georgia. I have not received a letter from any source since leaving Florida, and of course I am very lonesome and hunger terribly for the communion of friends. I will remain here eight or nine months and hope to hear from all my friends.

Fate and flowers have carried me to California, and I had reveled and luxuriated amid its plants and mountains nearly four months. I am well again. I came to life in the cool winds and crystal waters of the mountains, and were it not for a thought now and then of loneliness and isolation, the pleasure of my existence would be complete. . . .

The valley of the San Joaquin is the flower readiest piece of world I ever walked, one vast, level, even flower-bed, a sheet of flowers, the smooth sea ruffled a little by the tree fringing of the river and here and there of smaller cross streams from the mountains. Florida is indeed a land of flowers, but for every flower creature that dwells in its most delightsome places more than a hundred are living here. Here, here is Florida. . . .

I'm sorry my page is done. I have not told anything. I thought of you, Mrs. Carr, when I was in the glorious Yosemite, . . . that you would see it, and worship there. . . . It is by far the grandest of all the special temples of nature I was ever permitted to enter. It must be the *sanctum sanctorum* of the Sierras, and I trust that you will all be led to it.   —KRS, 71–74

Twenty Hill Hollow, August 15, 1868
Letter to Annie Muir

I am always a little lonesome, Annie. Ought I not to be a man by this time and put away childish things? I have wandered far enough and seen strange faces enough to feel the whole world a home, and I am a bachelor too. I should not be a boy, but I cannot accustom myself to the coldness of strangers, nor to the shiftings and wanderings of this Arab life.[55]

Jeanne Carr moved to Oakland in February 1869, when her husband took up a position at the University of California at Berkeley. Muir was still living a solitary existence in Twenty Hill Hollow, and Carr remonstrates with him not to remain indefinitely in isolation "lest your highest pleasures, taken selfishly, become impure." Carr visited Yosemite in 1870, but missed Muir, who was in the high country. During the next several years, Carr will repeatedly exhort Muir to find his way back into

*civilized life where he can offer his vision of a sacred wilder-
ness to the American public. "I could envy you your solitude,"*
she acknowledges, while cautioning him, *"but there may be too
much of it."*[56]

Twenty Hill Hollow, February 24, 1869
Letter to Jeanne Carr

Your two California notes from San Francisco and San Mateo
reached me last evening, and I rejoice at the glad tidings they
bring of your arrival in this magnificent land. I have thought
of you hundreds of times in my seasons of deepest joy, amid
the flower purple and gold of the plains, the fern fields in gorge
and canyon, the sacred waters, tree columns, and the eternal
unnameable sublimities of the mountains. Of all my friends, you
are the only one that understands my motives and enjoyments.

Only a few weeks ago a true liberal-minded friend sent me a
large sheet full of terrible blue-steel [religious] orthodoxy, calling me from clouds and flowers to the practical walks of politics
and philanthropy. Mrs. Carr, thought I, never lectured thus. I am
glad, indeed, that you were here to read for yourself these glorious lessons of sky and plain and mountain, which no mortal
power can ever speak. I thought when in the Yosemite Valley last
spring that the Lord had written things there that you would be
allowed to read sometime.

I am engaged at present in the very important and patriarchal
business of sheep. I am a gentle shepherd. The gray box in which
I reside is distant about seven miles northeast from Hopeton,
two miles north of Snelling. The Merced [River] pours past me
on the south from the Yosemite; smooth, domey hills and the
tree fringe of the Tuolumne [River] bound me on the north; the
lordly Sierras join the sky and plain on the east; and the far coast
mountains on the west. My mutton family of eighteen hundred
range over about ten miles, and I have abundant opportunities
for reading and botanizing. . . .   —KRS, 80–81

The following is excerpted from an article published in July 1872 in the Overland Monthly *and later revised by Muir. This revision was found in his literary effects and published by William Frederic Badè as the final chapter of* A Thousand-Mile Walk to the Gulf *(The full essay appears as chapter 6 of this volume.)*

Twenty Hill Hollow, Spring 1869

Never shall I forget my baptism in this font. It happened in January, the resurrection day for many a plant and for me. I suddenly found myself on one of its hills; the hollow overflowed with light, as a fountain, and only small, sunless nooks were kept for mosseries and ferneries. Hollow Creek spangled and mazed like a river. The ground steamed with fragrance. Light, of unspeakable richness, was brooding the flowers. Truly, said I, is California the Golden State—in metallic gold, in sun gold, and in planet gold. The sunshine for a whole summer seemed condensed into the chambers of that one glowing day. Every trace of bitterness had been washed from the sky; the mountains were dusted and wiped clean with clouds—Pacheco Peak and Mt. Diablo, and the waved blue wall between; the grand Sierra stood along the plain, colored in four horizontal bands; the lowest, rose purple; the next higher, dark purple; the next, blue; and, above all, the white row of summits pointing to the heavens.

It may be asked, what have mountains fifty or a hundred miles away to do with Twenty Hill Hollow? To lovers of the wild, these mountains are not one hundred miles away. Their spiritual power and the goodness of the sky make them here, as a circle of friends. They rise as a portion of the hilled walls of the hollow. You cannot feel yourself out-of-doors; plain, sky, and mountains ray beauty which you feel. You bathe in these spirit-beams, turning round and round, as if warming at a campfire. Presently you lose consciousness of your own separate existence: you blend with the landscape and become part and parcel of nature.

—TMW, 210–12

On June 3, 1869, Muir left for the pastures of the high Sierras accompanying a flock of two thousand sheep. His journal of this summer combines exacting descriptions and detailed sketches of the geology and plant life he observed, with haunting accounts of heightened moods that continue his spiritual transformation, constituting, in his own words, "a conversion, so complete and wholesome" that he can no longer recall his earlier "bondage" days.

Horseshoe Bend (1,500 feet above the Merced River) June 5, 1869

After gaining the open summit of this first bench, feeling the natural exhilaration due to the slight elevation of a thousand feet or so and the hopes excited concerning the outlook to be obtained, the magnificent section of the Merced Valley at what is called Horseshoe Bend came full in sight—a glorious wilderness that seemed to be calling with a thousand, songful voices. Bold, down-sweeping slopes, feathered with pines and clumps of manzanita with sunny, open spaces between them, make up most of the foreground; the middle and background present fold beyond fold of finely modeled hills and ridges rising into mountain-like masses in the distance. . . .

As far as the eye can reach it extends, a heaving, swelling sea of green . . . a grand congregation of massive heights with the river shining between. . . . The whole landscape showed design, like man's noblest sculptures. How wonderful the power of its beauty! Gazing awe-stricken, I might have left everything for it. Glad, endless work would then be mine tracing the forces that have brought forth its features, its rocks and plants and animals and glorious weather. Beauty beyond thought everywhere, beneath, above, made and being made forever. I gazed and gazed and longed and admired until the dusty sheep and packs were far out of sight, made hurried notes and a sketch, though there was no need for either, for the colors and lines and expression of this divine landscape countenance are so burned into my mind and heart, they surely can never grow dim.   —MFS, 17–19

Northwest of Yosemite Valley, June 6, 1869

Now we are fairly into the mountains, and they are into us. We are fairly living now. What bright seething white-fire enthusiasm is bred in us—without our help or knowledge. A perfect influx into every pore and cell of us, fusing, vaporizing by its heat until the boundary walls of our heavy flesh tabernacle seem taken down and we flow and diffuse into the very air and trees and streams and rocks, thrilling with them to the touch of the vital sunbeams. Responsive, we are part of nature now, neither old nor young, but immortal in a terrestrial way, neither sick nor well. . . .

How glorious a conversion, so complete and wholesome is it, scarce memory of old bondage days is left as a standpoint to view it from, even in the silence and darkness of the camp at night. We rather seem to have been so always. Nature like a fluid seems to drench and steep us throughout, as the whole sky and the rocks and flowers are drenched with spiritual life—with God. Now I am not longer a shepherd with a few bruised beans and crackers in my stomach and wrapped in a woolen blanket, but a free bit of everything, not to be defined as to extent nor cramped or bound as to movements more than clouds are.

What a glorious drift I enjoyed when looking through the yellow pines today. I caught sight of the snowy peaks grouped about the headwaters of the Merced River. How near they seemed and how clear their outlines on the blue air, or rather in the blue air, for they seemed saturated with the very substance of the sky. What promise they held out, and invitation, and how grand the attraction I felt. I would reach these sometime, I felt, and I would go to these in very love to learn whatever I might be able. Then it would all seem too good to be true. I would never be allowed so noble a duty—someone worthy would go and be blest. Yet will I drift about these mountains, movements of Divine love, near or far, here or there, willing—dearly loving to be but a servant of servants in this holy wilderness.[57]

Near Brown's Flat, northwest of Yosemite Valley June 14, 1869

One of these ancient flood-boulders stands firm in the middle of the stream channel, just below the lower edge of the pool dam at the foot of the fall nearest our camp. It is a nearly cubical mass of granite about eight feet high, plushed with mosses over the top and down the sides to ordinary high-water mark. When I climbed on top of it today and lay down to rest, it seemed the most romantic spot I had yet found—the one big stone with its mossy level top and smooth sides standing square and firm and solitary, like an altar, the fall in front of it bathing it lightly with the finest of the spray, just enough to keep its moss cover fresh. . . .

How soothingly, restfully cool it is beneath that leafy, trans-lucent ceiling, and how delightful the water music—deep bass tones of the fall, the clashing, ringing spray, and infinite variety of small, low tones of the current gliding past the side of the boulder island. . . . All this shut in; every one of these influences acting at short range as if in a quiet room. The place seemed holy, where one might hope to see God.

After dark, when the camp was at rest, I groped my way back to the altar boulder and passed the night on it—above the water, beneath the leaves and stars. . . . Precious night, precious day to abide in me forever. Thanks be to God for this immortal gift.

—MFS, 64–65

Near Brown's Flat, June 23, 1869

Oh, these vast, calm, measureless mountain days, inciting at once to work and rest! Days in whose light everything seems equally divine, opening a thousand windows to show us God.

Nevermore, however weary, should one faint by the way who gains the blessings of one mountain day; whatever his fate, long life, short life, stormy life or calm, he is rich forever.

—MFS, 82

Near Brown's Flat, June 30, 1869

And so this memorable month ends, a stream of beauty unmeasured, no more to be sectioned off by almanac arithmetic than sun radiance, or the currents of seas and rivers—a peaceful, joyful stream of beauty. Every morning, arising from the death of sleep, the happy plants and all our fellow animal creatures great and small, and even the rocks, seemed to be shouting, "Awake, awake, rejoice, rejoice, come love us and join in our song. Come! Come!" Looking back through the stillness and romantic, enchanting beauty and peace of the grove, this June seems the greatest of all the months of my life, the most truly, divinely free, boundless like eternity, immortal. Everything in it seems equally divine—one smooth, pure, wild glow of Heaven's love, never to be blotted or blurred by anything past or to come.

—MFS, 90

Near Brown's Flat, July 2, 1869

Warm, sunny day, thrilling plant and animals and rocks alike, making sap and blood flow fast, and making every particle of the crystal mountains throb and swirl and dance in glad accord like stardust. No dullness anywhere visible or thinkable. No stagnation, no death. Everything kept in joyful rhythmic motion in the pulses of Nature's big heart.   —MFS, 98

Near Brown's Flat, July 5, 1869

The clouds of noon on the high Sierra seem yet more marvelously, indescribably beautiful from day to day as one becomes more wakeful to see them. . . . Here, every day is a holiday, a jubilee ever sounding with serene enthusiasm, without wear or waste or cloying weariness. Everything rejoicing. Not a single cell or crystal unvisited or forgotten. —MFS, 100–101

Near Brown's, Flat July 7, 1869

Rather weak and sickish this morning, and all about a piece of bread. [Muir's employer, "The Don," was late in bringing provisions to the shepherds.] Can scarce command attention to my best studies, as if one couldn't take a few days' saunter in the Godful woods without maintaining a base on a wheat field and gristmill. . . . Bread without flesh is a good diet, as on many botanical excursions I have proved. Tea also may easily be ignored. Just bread and water in delightful toil is all I need—not unreasonably much, yet one ought to be trained and tempered to enjoy life in these brave wilds in full, independent of any particular kind of nourishment. . . . Drank tea until half intoxicated. Man seems to crave a stimulant when anything extraordinary is going on, and this is the only one I use. Billy chews great quantities of tobacco, which I suppose helps to stupefy and moderate his misery. We look and listen for the Don every hour. How beautiful upon the mountains his big feet would be!

At last Don Delaney comes down the lang glen—hunger vanishes, we turn our eyes to the mountains, and tomorrow go climbing toward cloudland. Never while anything is left of me shall this first camp be forgotten. It has fairly grown into me, not merely as memory pictures, but as part and parcel of mind and body alike. The deep hopper-like hollow, with its majestic trees through which all the wonderful nights the stars poured their beauty. . . .

And the dawns and sunrises and sundowns of these mountain days—the rose light creeping higher among the stars, changing to daffodil yellow, the level beams bursting forth, streaming across the ridges, touching pine after pine, awakening and warming all the mighty host to do gladly their shining day's work. The great sun-gold noons, the alabaster cloud-mountains, the landscape beaming with consciousness like the face of a god. The sunsets, when the trees stood hushed awaiting their good night blessings. Divine, enduring, unwastable wealth.   —MFS, 103–13

The following passage is an example of Muir's ability to effort-
lessly fuse the empirical and the spiritual. While still aglow
from his immersion in a world where the mountains and for-
ests appear "equally divine," his empirical eye—apparently for
the first time—notices evidence of glacial activity—large boul-
ders deposited randomly across the high Sierra landscape, their
granite faces polished and scored by passing ice fields—phenom-
ena that will set in motion his theory of the glacial origins of
Yosemite.

Near Tamarack Flat, July 11, 1869

We are now about 7,000 feet above the sea, and the nights are so cool we have to pile coats and extra clothing on top of our blankets. Tamarack Creek is icy cold, delicious, exhilarating champagne water. It is flowing bank full in the meadow with silent speed, but only a few hundred yards below our camp the ground is bare gray granite strewn with boulders . . . [the boulders] lying so still and deserted with no moving force near them, no boulder carrier anywhere in sight, were nevertheless brought from a distance, as difference in color and composition shows, quarried and carried and laid down here each in its place . . . strangers in a strange land.

And with what tools were they quarried and carried? On the pavement we find its marks. The most resisting, unweathered portion of the surface is scored and striated in a rigidly parallel way, indicating that the region has been over swept by a glacier from the northeastward, grinding down the general mass of the mountains, scoring and polishing, producing a strange, raw, wiped appearance, and dropping whatever boulders it chanced to be carrying at the time it was melted at the close of the Glacial Period. A fine discovery this. . . .

All the Merced streams are wonderful singers, and the Yosemite is the center where the main tributaries meet. From a point about half a mile from our camp we can see into the lower end of the famous valley, with its wonderful cliffs and groves, and grand pages of mountain manuscript that I would gladly give my life to be able to read. . . .

Have greatly enjoyed all this huge day, sauntering and seeing, steeping in the mountain influences, sketching, noting, pressing flowers, drinking ozone and Tamarack water. . . . Sauntered up the meadow about sundown, out of sight of camp and sheep and all human mark, into the deep peace of the solemn old woods, everything glowing with Heaven's unquenchable enthusiasm.

—MFS, 132–37

North of Yosemite Valley, Summer 1869
Letter to Sarah Muir Galloway

Just think of the blessedness of my lot!—have been camped here, right in the midst of Yosemite rocks and waters for fifteen days, with nearly all of every day to myself to climb, sketch, write, meditate, and botanize! My foot has pressed no floor but that of the mountains for many a day. I am far from the ways and pursuits of man. I seldom even hear the bleating of our two thousand sheep. The manifold overwhelming sublimities of the Sierra are all in all. I am with Nature in the grandest, most divine of all her earthly dwelling places. . . .

A few months will call upon me to decide to what portion of God's glorious star I will next turn. The sweets of home, the smooth waters of civilized life have attractions for me whose power is increased by time and constant rambling, but I am a captive, I am bound. Love of pure unblemished Nature seems to overmaster and blur out of sight all other objects and considerations. I know that I could under ordinary circumstances

accumulate wealth and obtain a fair position in society, and I am
arrived at an age that requires that I should choose some definite
course for life. But I am sure that the mind of no truant school-
boy is more free and disengaged from all the grave plans and
purposes and pursuits of ordinary orthodox life than mine. But I
wonder what spirit is conjuring up such sober affairs at this time.
I only meant to say a word by way of family greeting. Tomorrow I will be among the sublimities of Yosemite and forget that
ever a thought of civilization or time-honored proprieties came
among my pathless, lawless thoughts and wanderings.

                                                          —LL, 1:203–4

*The following passage describes one of Muir's more celebrated
escapades, when he climbs down into Yosemite Creek and out
over the brink of Yosemite Falls where it plunges three thousand feet into the valley below. In the intensity of the experience
Muir loses all sense of time and is so "nerve shaken" by it that
his sleep is disturbed by dreams of geologic catastrophe. One
time, springing to his feet, he cried, "This time it is real—all
must die."*[58]

North of Yosemite Valley, July 15, 1869

After luncheon I made haste to high ground, and from the top of
the ridge on the west side of Indian Canyon I gained the noblest
view of the summit peaks I have ever yet enjoyed. Nearly all
the upper basin of the Merced was displayed, with its sublime
domes and canyons, dark upsweeping forests, and glorious array
of white peaks deep in the sky, every feature glowing, radiating
beauty that pours into our flesh and bones like heat rays from
fire. Sunshine over all; no breath of wind to stir the brooding
calm. Never before had I seen so glorious a landscape, so boundless an affluence of sublime mountain beauty. The most extravagant description I might give of this view to anyone who has not
seen similar landscapes with his own eyes would not so much as

hint its grandeur and the spiritual glow that covered it. I shouted and gesticulated in a wild burst of ecstasy, much to the astonishment of St. Bernard Carlo, who came running up to me, manifesting in his intelligent eyes a puzzled concern that was very ludicrous, which had the effect of bringing me to my senses. . . .

I rambled along the valley rim to the westward; most of it is rounded off on the very brink, so that it is not easy to find places where one may look clear down the face of the wall to the bottom [of Yosemite Valley]. When such places were found, and I had cautiously set my feet and drawn my body erect, I could not help fearing a little that the rock might split off and let me down, and what a down—more than three thousand feet. Still my limbs did not tremble, nor did I feel the least uncertainty as to the reliance to be placed on them. My only fear was that a flake of the granite, which in some places showed joints more or less open and running parallel with the face of the cliff, might give way. After withdrawing from such places, excited with the view I had got, I would say to myself, "Now don't go out on the verge again." But in the face of Yosemite scenery cautious remonstrance is vain; under its spell one's body seems to go where it likes with a will over which we seem to have scarce any control.

After a mile or so of this memorable cliff work, I approached Yosemite Creek, admiring its easy, graceful, confident gestures as it comes bravely forward in its narrow channel, singing the last of its mountain songs on its way to its fate—a few rods more over the shining granite, then down half a mile in snowy foam to another world, to be lost in the Merced [River], where climate, vegetation, inhabitants, all are different. Emerging from its last gorge, it glides in wide lace-like rapids down a smooth incline into a pool where it seems to rest and compose its gray, agitated waters before taking the grand plunge [into the Valley]. Then slowly slipping over the lip of the pool basin, it descends another glossy slope with rapidly accelerated speed to the brink of the tremendous cliff, and with sublime, fateful confidence springs out free in the air.

I took off my shoes and stockings and worked my way cautiously down alongside the rushing flood, keeping my feet and hands pressed firmly on the polished rock. The booming, roaring water, rushing past close to my head, was very exciting. I had expected that the sloping apron would terminate with the perpendicular wall of the valley, and that from the foot of it, where it is less steeply inclined, I should be able to lean far enough out to see the forms and behavior of the fall all the way down to the bottom. But I found that there was yet another small brow over which I could not see, and which appeared to be too steep for mortal feet. Scanning it keenly, I discovered a narrow shelf about three inches wide on the very brink, just wide enough for a rest for one's heels. But there seemed to be no way of reaching it over so steep a brow. At length, after careful scrutiny of the surface, I found an irregular edge of a flake of the rock some distance back from the margin of the torrent. If I was to get down to the brink at all, that rough edge, which might offer slight finger holds, was the only way. But the slope beside it looked dangerously smooth and steep, and the swift roaring flood beneath, overhead, and beside me was very nerve-trying. I therefore concluded not to venture farther, but did nevertheless. Tufts of artemisia were growing in clefts of the rock nearby, and I filled my mouth with the bitter leaves, hoping they might help to prevent giddiness. Then, with a caution not known in ordinary circumstances, I crept down safely to the little ledge, got my heels well planted on it, then shuffled in a horizontal direction twenty or thirty feet until close to the out plunging current, which, by the time it had descended thus far, was already white. Here I obtained a perfectly free view down into the heart of the snowy, chanting throng of comet-like streamers, into which the body of the fall soon separates.

While perched on that narrow niche I was not distinctly conscious of danger. The tremendous grandeur of the fall in form and sound and motion, acting at close range, smothered the sense of fear, and in such places one's body takes keen care for safety on its own account. How long I remained down there, or how I returned, I can hardly tell. Anyhow I had a glorious time and got back to camp about dark, enjoying triumphant exhilaration soon followed by dull weariness. Hereafter I'll try to keep from such extravagant, nerve-straining places. Yet such a day is well worth venturing for. My first view of the High Sierra, first view looking down into Yosemite, the death song of Yosemite Creek, and its flight over the vast cliff, each one of these is of itself enough for a great life-long landscape fortune—a most memorable day of days—enjoyment enough to kill if that were possible.   —MFS, 152–60

North of Yosemite Valley, July 16, 1869

My enjoyments yesterday afternoon, especially at the head of the fall, were too great for good sleep. Kept starting up last night in a nervous tremor, half awake, fancying that the foundation of the mountain we were camped on had given way and was falling into Yosemite Valley. In vain I roused myself to make a new beginning for sound sleep. The nerve strain had been too great, and again and again I dreamed I was rushing through the air above a glorious avalanche of water and rocks. One time, springing to my feet, I said, "This time it is real—all must die, and where could a mountaineer find a more glorious death!"
                                                        —MFS, 160–61

North of Yosemite Valley, July 19, 1869

Watching the daybreak and sunrise. The pale rose and purple sky changing softly to daffodil yellow and white, sunbeams pouring through the passes between the peaks and over the Yosemite domes, making their edges burn; the silver firs in the middle ground catching the glow on their spiry tops, and our camp grove fills and thrills with the glorious light. Everything awakening, alert and joyful; the birds begin to stir and innumerable insect people. Deer quietly withdraw into leafy hiding places in the chaparral; the dew vanishes, flowers spread their petals, every pulse beats high, every life cell rejoices, the very rocks seem to thrill with life. The whole landscape glows like a human face in the glory of enthusiasm, and the blue sky, pale around the horizon, bends peacefully down over all like one vast flower. . . .

About noon, as usual, big bossy cumuli began to grow above the forest, and the rainstorm pouring from them is the most imposing I have yet seen. The silvery zigzag lightning lances are longer than usual, and the thunder gloriously impressive, keen, crashing, intensely concentrated, speaking with such tremendous energy it would seem that an entire mountain is being shattered at every stroke, but probably only a few trees are being shattered, many of which I have seen on my walks hereabouts strewing the ground. . . . Now comes the rain, with corresponding extravagant grandeur, covering the ground high and low with a sheet of flowing water, a transparent film fitted like a skin upon the rugged anatomy of the landscape, making the rocks glitter and glow, gathering in the ravines, flooding the streams, and making them shout and boom in reply to the thunder. . . .

Happy the showers that fall on so fair a wilderness—scarce a single drop can fail to find a beautiful spot—on the tops of the peaks, on the shining glacier pavements, on the great smooth domes, on forests and gardens and brushy moraines, plashing, glinting, pattering, laving . . . good luck and good work for the happy mountain raindrops, each one of them a high waterfall in itself, descending from the cliffs and hollows of the clouds to the cliffs and hollows of the rocks, out of sky thunder into the thunder of the falling rivers. . . .

Now the storm is over, the sky is clear, the last rolling thunder-wave is spent on the peaks, and where are the raindrops now—what has become of all the shining throng? In winged vapor rising, some are already hastening back to the sky, some have gone to the plants, creeping through invisible doors into the round rooms of cells, some are locked in crystals of ice, some in rock crystals, some in porous moraines to keep their small springs flowing, some have gone journeying on in the rivers to join the larger raindrop of the ocean. From form to form, beauty to beauty, ever-changing, never resting, all are speeding on with love's enthusiasm, singing with the stars the eternal song of creation. —MFS, 164–70

North of Yosemite Valley, July 20, 1869

Fine calm morning; air tense and clear; not the slightest breeze astir; everything shining, the rocks with wet crystals, the plants with dew, each receiving its portion of irised dewdrops and sunshine, like living creatures getting their breakfast, their dew manna coming down from the starry sky like swarms of smaller stars. . . .

By the time the sun is fairly above the mountaintops, I am beyond the flock, free to rove and revel in the wilderness all the big immortal days. . . . No pain here, no dull empty hours, no fear of the past, no fear of the future. These blessed mountains are so compactly filled with God's beauty, no petty personal hope or experience has room to be. Drinking this champagne water is pure pleasure, so is breathing the living air, and every movement of limbs is a pleasure, while the whole body seems to feel beauty when exposed to it as it feels the campfire or sunshine, entering, not by the eyes alone, but equally through all one's flesh like radiant heat, making a passionate ecstatic pleasure-glow not explainable. One's body then seems homogenous throughout, sound as a crystal.

Perched like a fly on this Yosemite dome [North dome], I gaze
and sketch and bask . . . humbly prostrate before the vast display
of God's power, and eager to offer self-denial and renunciation
with eternal toil to learn any lesson in the divine manuscript. . . .

Now the sun breaks forth and fragrant steam rises. The West
is flaming in gold and purple, ready for the ceremony of the sunset, and back I go to camp with my notes and pictures, the best
of them printed in my mind as dreams. A fruitful day, without
measured beginning or ending. A terrestrial eternity. A gift of
good God. . . .

The deeper the solitudes the less the sense of loneliness, and
the nearer our friends. Now bread and tea, for bed and good-
night to Carlo (the St. Bernard), a look at the sky lilies, and
death sleep until the dawn of another Sierra tomorrow.

—MFS, 170–78

Near Tuolumne Meadows, July 24, 1869

Clouds at noon, occupying about half the sky gave half an
hour of heavy rain to wash one of the cleanest landscapes in
the world. How well it is washed! . . . A few minutes ago every
tree was excited, bowing to the roaring storm, waiting, swirling,
tossing their branches in glorious enthusiasm like worship. But
though to the outer ear these trees are now silent, their songs
never cease. Every hidden cell is throbbing with music and life,
every fiber thrilling like harp strings, while incense is ever flowing from the balsam bells and leaves. No wonder the hills and
groves were God's first temples, and the more they are cut down,
and hewn into cathedrals and churches, the farther off and dim-
mer seems the Lord himself. The same may be said of stone
temples.

Yonder, to the eastward of our camp grove, stands one of
nature's cathedrals, hewn from the living rock, almost conventional in form, about 2,000 feet high, nobly adorned with spires
and pinnacles, thrilling under floods of sunshine as if alive like a

grove temple, and well named "Cathedral Peak." Even Shepherd Billy turns at times to this wonderful mountain building, though apparently deaf to all stone sermons. Snow that refused to melt in fire would hardly be more wonderful than unchanging dullness in the rays of God's beauty. I have been trying to get him to walk to the brink of Yosemite for a view, offering to watch the sheep for a day, while he should enjoy what tourists come from all over the world to see. But though within a mile of the famous Valley, he will not go to it, even out of mere curiosity. "What," says he, "is Yosemite but a Canyon—a lot of rocks—a hole in the ground—a place dangerous about falling into—a damned good place to keep away from."

"But think of the waterfalls, Billy—just think of that big stream we crossed the other day, falling half a mile through the air—think of that, and the sound it makes. You can hear it now like the roar of the sea."

Thus I pressed Yosemite upon him like a missionary offering the gospel, but he would have none of it. . . .   —MFS, 195–97

North of Yosemite Valley, July 26, 1869

Ramble to the summit of Mt. Hoffman, 11,000 feet high, the highest point in life's journey my feet have yet touched. And what glorious landscapes are about me, new plants, new animals, new crystals, and multitudes of new mountains, far higher than Hoffman, towering in glorious array along the axis of the range, serene, majestic, snow-laden, sun-drenched, vast domes and ridges shining below them, forests, lakes, and meadows in the hollows, the pure blue bellflower sky brooding over them all—a glory day of admission into a new realm of wonders, as if nature had wooingly whispered, "come higher." What questions I asked, and how little I know of all the vast show, and how eagerly, tremulously hopeful of someday knowing more, learning the meaning of these divine symbols crowded together on this wondrous page. . . .

How boundless the day seems as we revel in the storm-beaten sky gardens amid so vast a congregation of on-looking mountains! . . . The surface of the ground, so dull and forbidding at first sight, besides being rich in plants, shines and sparkles with crystals: mica, hornblende, feldspar, quartz, tourmaline. The radiance in some places is so great as to be fairly dazzling, keen lance rays of every color flashing, sparkling in glorious abundance, joining the plants and their fine, brave beauty work— every crystal, every flower a window opening into heaven, a mirror reflecting the creator.

From garden to garden, ridge to ridge, I drifted, enchanted, now on my knees gazing into the face of a daisy, now climbing again and again among the purple and azure flowers of the hemlocks, now down into the treasuries of the snow, or gazing afar over domes, and peaks, lakes and woods, and the billowy, glaciated fields of the upper Tuolumne, and trying to sketch them. In the midst of such beauty, pierced with its rays, one's body is all one tingling palette. Who wouldn't be a Mountaineer! Up here all the world's prizes seem nothing. . . .

All these come to mind, as well as the plant people, and the glad streams singing their way to the sea. But most impressive of all is the vast glowing countenance of the wilderness in awful, infinite repose.

Toward sunset, enjoyed a fine run to camp, down the long south slopes, across ridges and ravines, gardens and avalanche gaps, through the firs and chaparral, enjoying wild excitement and excess of strength, and so ends a day that will never end.

—MFS, 199–209

Tenaya Lake, July 27, 1869

Up and away to Lake Tenaya—another big day, enough for a lifetime. The rocks, the air, everything speaking with audible voice or silent; joyful, wonderful, enchanting, banishing weariness and sense of time. No longing for anything now or hereafter as we go home into the mountains' heart. . . .

Many mossy emerald bogs, meadows, and gardens in rocky hollows to wade and saunter through—and what fine plants they give me, what joyful streams I have to cross, and how many views are displayed of the Hoffman and Cathedral peak masonry, and what a wondrous breadth of shining granite pavement to walk over for the first time about the shores of the lake! On I sauntered in freedom complete; body without weight as far as I was aware. . . .

No Sierra landscape that I have seen holds anything truly dead or dull, or any trace of what in manufactories is called rubbish or waste; everything is perfectly clean and pure and full of divine lessons. This quick, inevitable interest attaching to everything seems marvelous until the hand of God becomes visible; then it seems reasonable that what interests Him may well interest us. When we try to pick out anything by itself, we find it hitched to everything else in the universe. One fancies a heart like our own must be beating in every crystal and cell, and we feel like stopping to speak to the plants and animals as friendly, fellow mountaineers. —MFS, 209–11

For Muir, the "natural and common" held far more mystery than psychic phenomena like telepathy or "spirit-rapping," which were much in vogue during this period. Yet, he occasionally experienced moments of telepathic communication which his empirical self could not account for—premonitions, for instance, of both his father's and mother's deaths, which caused him to immediately take a train back to the Midwest and join them in their final hours.

The following excerpt describes one such episode, when Muir, sketching in the late afternoon on North Dome, several thousand feet above Yosemite Valley, suddenly felt the presence of his mentor, Professor James Butler, from the University of Wisconsin, whom he had not seen since he had left Madison. The sensation was palpable enough to send Muir down into the valley the following morning, a three-thousand-foot descent (there were no trails), where he found the professor, to the amazement of both of them.

North of Yosemite Valley, August 2, 1869

Clouds and showers, about the same as yesterday. Sketching all day on the North Dome until four or five o'clock in the afternoon, when, as I was busily employed thinking only of the glorious Yosemite landscape, trying to draw every tree and every line and feature of the rocks, I was suddenly, and without warning, possessed with the notion that my friend, Professor J. D. Butler, of the State University of Wisconsin, was below me in the valley, and I jumped up full of the idea of meeting him, with almost as much startling excitement as if he had suddenly touched me to make me look up. Leaving my work without the slightest deliberation, I ran down the western slope of the Dome and along the brink of the valley wall, looking for a way to the bottom, until I came to a side canyon, which, judging by its apparently continuous growth of trees and bushes, I thought might afford a practical way into the valley, and immediately began to make the descent, late as it was, as if drawn irresistibly.

But after a little, common sense stopped me and explained that it would be long after dark ere I could possibly reach the hotel, that the visitors would be asleep, that nobody would know me, that I had no money in my pockets, and moreover was without a coat. I therefore compelled myself to stop, and finally succeeded in reasoning myself out of the notion of seeking my friend in the dark, whose presence I only felt in a strange, telepathic way. I succeeded in dragging myself back through the woods to camp, never for a moment wavering, however, in my determination to go down to him next morning. This I think is the most unexplainable notion that ever struck me. Had someone whispered in my ear while I sat on the Dome, where I had spent so many days, that Professor Butler was in the valley, I could not have been more surprised and startled.

When I was leaving the university he said, "Now, John, I want to hold you in sight and watch your career. Promise to write me at least once a year." I received a letter from him in July, at our first camp in the Hollow, written in May, in which he said that he might possibly visit California sometime this summer, and therefore hoped to meet me. But inasmuch as he named no meeting-place, and gave no directions as to the course he would probably follow, and as I should be in the wilderness all summer, I had not the slightest hope of seeing him, and all thought of the matter had vanished from my mind until this afternoon, when he seemed to be wafted bodily almost against my face. Well, to-morrow I shall see; for, reasonable or unreasonable, I feel I must go.   —MFS, 238–41

North of Yosemite Valley, August 3, 1869

Had a wonderful day. Found Professor Butler as the compass-needle finds the pole. So last evening's telepathy, transcendental revelation, or whatever else it may be called, was true; for, strange to say, he had just entered the valley by way of the Coulterville Trail and was coming up the valley past El Capitan when his presence struck me. Had he then looked toward the North Dome with a good glass when it first came in sight, he might have seen me jump up from my work and run toward him. This seems the one well-defined marvel of my life of the kind called supernatural; for, absorbed in glad Nature, spirit-rappings, second sight, ghost stories, etc., have never interested me since boyhood, seeming comparatively useless and infinitely less wonderful than Nature's open, harmonious, songful, sunny, everyday beauty. . . .

[After locating the professor near Vernal Falls] I stood directly in front of him, looked him in the face, and held out my hand. He thought I was offering to assist him in rising. "Never mind," he said. Then I said, "Professor Butler, don't you know me?" "I think not," he replied; but catching my eye, sudden recognition followed, and astonishment that I should have found him just when he was lost in the brush and did not know that I was within hundreds of miles of him. "John Muir, John Muir, where have you come from?"

Then I told him the story of my feeling his presence when he entered the valley last evening, when he was four or five miles distant, as I sat sketching on the North Dome. This, of course, only made him wonder the more. . . .

As we sat at dinner [at the hotel], the General [Benjamin Alvord, a guest] leaned back in his chair, and looking down the table, thus introduced me to the dozen guests or so, including the staring fisherman mentioned above: "This man, you know, came down out of these huge, trackless mountains, you know, to find his friend Professor Butler here, the very day he arrived; and how did he know he was here? He just felt him, he says. This is the queerest case of Scotch farsightedness I ever heard of," etc., etc. While my friend quoted Shakespeare: "More things in heaven and earth, Horatio, than are dreamt of in your philosophy. . . ."

—MFS, 241–49

North of Yosemite Valley, August 4, 1869

It seemed strange to sleep in a paltry hotel chamber after the spacious magnificence and luxury of the starry sky and silver fir grove . . . Calling Carlo, I scrambled home through the Indian Canon gate, rejoicing, pitying the poor Professor and General, bound by clocks, almanacs, orders, duties, etc., and compelled to dwell with lowland care and dust and din, where Nature is covered and her voice smothered, while the poor, insignificant wanderer enjoys the freedom and glory of God's wilderness. . . .

It seems strange that visitors to Yosemite should be so little influenced by its novel grandeur, as if their eyes were bandaged and their ears stopped. Most of those I saw yesterday were looking down as if wholly unconscious of anything going on about them, while the sublime rocks were trembling with the tones of the mighty chanting congregation of waters gathered from all the mountains round about, making music that might draw angels out of heaven. . . .

Now I'm back at the camp-fire, and cannot help thinking about my recognition of my friend's presence in the valley while he was four or five miles away, and while I had no means of knowing that he was not thousands of miles away. It seems supernatural, but only because it is not understood. Anyhow, it seems silly to make so much of it, while the natural and common is more truly marvelous and mysterious than the so-called supernatural. Indeed most of the miracles we hear of are infinitely less wonderful than the commonest of natural phenomena, when fairly seen. Perhaps the invisible rays that struck me while I sat at work on the Dome are something like those which attract and repel people at first sight, concerning which so much nonsense has been written. The worst apparent effect of these mysterious odd things is blindness to all that is divinely common. . . .

—MFS, 250–57

Near Tuolumne Meadows, August 14, 1869

On the way back to our Tuolumne camp, I enjoyed the scenery if possible more than when it first came into view. . . . The forests, too, seem kindly familiar, and the lakes and meadows and glad singing streams. I should like to dwell with them forever. Here with bread and water I should be content. Even if not allowed to roam and climb, tethered to a stake or tree in some meadow or grove, even then I should be content forever. Bathed in such beauty, watching the expressions ever varying on the faces of the mountains, watching the stars, which here have a glory that the low lander never dreams of, watching the circling seasons, listening to the songs of the waters and winds and birds, would be endless pleasure. And what glorious cloudlands I should see, storms and columns—a new heaven and a new earth every day. . . . One would be at an endless Godful play, and what speeches and music and acting and scenery and lights!—sun, moon, stars, auroras, creation just beginning, the morning stars "still singing together and all the sons of God shouting for joy."

—MFS, 286–87

Near Tuolumne Meadows, August 21, 1869

Early in the morning I tied my notebook and some bread to my belt and strode away full of eager hope, feeling that I was going to have a glorious revel. The glacier meadows that lay along my way served to smooth my morning speed. . . . In this fine company, sauntering enchanted, taking no heed of time, I at length entered the gate of the past, and the huge rocks began to close around me in all their mysterious impressiveness. . . .

How the day passed I hardly know. By the map I have come only about ten or twelve miles and the sun is already low in the west showing how long I must've lingered, observing, sketching, taking notes among the glaciated rocks and moraines and alpine flowerbeds. At sundown the somber crags and peaks were inspired with the ineffable beauty of the alpenglow, and the solemn, awful stillness hushed everything in the landscape. . . .

Reading these grand mountain manuscripts displayed through every vicissitude of heat and cold, calm and storm, upheaving volcanoes and down-grinding glaciers, we see that everything in nature called destruction must be creation—a change from beauty to beauty.   —MFS, 289–308

Near Tuolumne Meadows, August 27, 1869

Contemplating the lace-like fabric of streams outspread over the mountains, we are reminded that everything is flowing—going somewhere, animals and so-called lifeless rocks as well as water. Thus the snow flows fast or slow in grand beauty making glaciers and avalanches; the area's majestic floods carrying minerals, plants, leaves, seeds, spores, with streams of music, and fragrance; water streams carrying rocks both in solution and in the form of mud particles, sand, pebbles, and boulders. Rocks flow from volcanoes like water from springs, and animals flock together and flow in currents modified by stepping, leaping, gliding, flying, swimming, etc. While the stars go streaming through space pulsed on and on forever like blood globules and Nature's warm heart.   —MFS, 316–17

Near Tuolumne Meadows, August 29, 1869

Bland, serene Indian summer weather. Have been gazing all day at the mountains, watching the changing lights. More and more plainly are they clothed with light as a garment, white-tinged with pale purple, palest during the midday hours, richest in the morning and evening. Everything seems consciously peaceful, thoughtful, faithfully waiting God's will.   —MFS, 318

Near Tuolumne Meadows, August 30, 1869

This day just like yesterday. A few clouds motionless and apparently with no work to do beyond looking beautiful. Frost enough for crystal building—glorious fields of ice-diamonds destined to last but a night. How lavish is Nature building, pulling down, creating, destroying, chasing every material particle from form to form, ever changing, ever beautiful.

Mr. Delaney arrived this morning. Felt not a trace of loneliness while he was gone. On the contrary, I never enjoyed grander company. The whole wilderness seems to be alive and familiar, full of humanity. The very stones seem talkative, sympathetic, brotherly. No wonder when we consider that we all have the same father and mother.   —MFS, 318–19

Near Tuolumne Meadows, August 31, 1869

Silky, cirrus wisps and fringes so fine they almost escape notice. Frost enough for another crop of crystals on the meadows, but none on the forests. . . . Every day opens and closes like a flower, noiseless, effortless. Divine peace glows on all the majestic landscape like a silent enthusiastic joy that sometimes transfigures a noble human face.   —MFS, 319

Near Tuolumne Meadows, September 1, 1869

Day all calm, another grand throb of nature's heart, ripening late flowers and seeds for next summer, full of life and the thoughts and plans of life to come, and full of ripe and ready death, beautiful as life, telling of divine wisdom and goodness and immortality. . . .

Far up the moraine-covered slopes and among crumbling rocks, I found many delicate, hardy plants, some of them still in flower. The best gains of this trip were the lessons of unity and interrelation of all the features of the landscape revealed in general views. The lakes and meadows are located just where the ancient glaciers bore heaviest at the foot of the steepest parts of their channels. . . . Every rock, mountain, stream, plant, lake, lawn, forest, garden, bird, beast, insect seems to call and invite us to come and learn something of its history and relationship. . . .

Soon I'll be going to the lowlands. The bread camp must soon be removed. If I had a few sacks of flour, an axe, and some matches, I would build a cabin of pine logs, pile up plenty of firewood about it and stay all winter to see the grand fertile snowstorms, watch the birds and animals that winter thus, how they live, how the forests look, snow laden or buried, and how the avalanches look and sound on their way down the mountains. But now I have to go, for there is nothing to spare in the way of provisions. I will surely be back, however, surely I'll be back. No other place has ever so overwhelmingly attracted me as this hospitable, Godful wilderness.   —MFS, 320–24

Near Tuolumne Meadows, September 2, 1869

A grand, red, rosy, crimson day—a perfect glory of a day. What it means I don't know. . . . One is constantly reminded of the infinite lavishness and fertility of nature—inexhaustible abundance amid what seems enormous waste. And yet when we look into any of her operations that lie within reach of our minds, we learn that no particle of her material is wasted or worn out. It is eternally flowing from use to use, beauty to yet higher beauty; and we soon cease to lament waste and death, and rather rejoice and exult in the imperishable, unspendable wealth of the universe, and faithfully watch and wait the reappearance of everything that melts and fades and dies about us, feeling sure that its next appearance will be better and more beautiful than the last. . . . More and more, in a place like this, we feel ourselves part of wild nature, kin to everything.   —MFS, 324–26

Near Tuolumne Meadows, September 6, 1869

Still another perfectly cloudless day, purple evening and morning, all the middle hours one mass of pure serene sunshine. Soon after sunrise the air grew warm, and there was no wind. One naturally halted to see what Nature intended to do. . . .

Mr. Delaney now keeps up a solemn talk about the need of getting away from these high mountains, telling sad stories of flocks that perished in storms that broke suddenly into the midst of fine innocent weather like this we are now enjoying. "In no case," said he, "will I venture to stay so high and far back in the mountains as we now are later than the middle of this month, no matter how warm and sunny it may be." He would move the flock slowly at first, a few miles a day until the Yosemite Creek basin was reached and crossed, then while lingering in the heavy pine woods should the weather threaten he could hurry down to the foothills, where the snow never falls deep enough to smother a sheep. Of course I am anxious to see as much of the wilderness as possible in the few days left me, and I say again—May the good time come, when I can stay as long as I like with plenty of bread, far and free from trampling flocks, though I may well be thankful for this generous inspiring summer. Anyhow we never know where we must go nor what guidance we are to get—men, storms, Guardian Angels, or sheep. Perhaps almost everybody in the least natural is guided more than he is ever aware of. All the wilderness seems to be full of tricks and plans to drive and draw us up into God's light.   —MFS, 329–31

September 7, 1869, near Tuolumne Meadows

Left camp at daybreak and made direct for Cathedral Peak, intending to strike eastward and southward from that point among the peaks and ridges at the heads of the Tuolumne, Merced, and San Joaquin rivers. Down through the pine woods I made my way, across the Tuolumne River and meadows, and up the heavily timbered slope forming the south boundary of the upper Tuolumne basin, along the east side of Cathedral Peak, and up to its topmost spire, which I reached at noon, having loitered by the way to study the fine trees—two-leaved pine, mountain pine, *albicaulis* pine, silver fir, and the most charming, most graceful of all the evergreens, the mountain hemlock. High, cool, late-flowering meadows also detained me, and lakelets and avalanche tracks and huge quarries of moraine rocks above the forests. . . .

The Cathedral is said to be about eleven thousand feet above the sea, but the height of the building itself above the level of the ridge it stands on is about fifteen hundred feet. A mile or so to the westward there is a handsome lake, and the glacier-polished granite about it is shining so brightly it is not easy in some places to trace. . . . No feature, however, of all the noble landscape as seen from here seems more wonderful than the Cathedral itself, a temple displaying Nature's best masonry and sermons in stones. How often I have gazed at it from the tops of hills and ridges, and through openings in the forests on my many short excursions, devoutly wondering, admiring, longing! This I may say is the first time I have been at church in California, led here at last, every door graciously opened for the poor lonely worshiper. In our best times everything turns into religion, all the world seems a church and the mountains altars. . . .

Camped beside a little pool and a group of crinkled dwarf pines; and as I sit by the fire trying to write notes the shallow pool seems fathomless with the infinite starry heavens in it, while the onlooking rocks and trees, tiny shrubs and daisies and sedges, brought forward in the fire-glow, seem full of thought as if about to speak aloud and tell all their wild stories. A marvelously impressive meeting in which everyone has something worthwhile to tell. And beyond the fire-beams out in the solemn darkness, how impressive is the music of a choir of rills singing their way down from the snow to the river! . . .

How delightful it is to be alone here! How wild everything is—wild as the sky and as pure! Never shall I forget this big, divine day—the Cathedral and its thousands of Cassiope bells, and the landscapes around them, and this camp in the gray crags above the woods, with its stars and streams and snow.

—MFS, 331–39

Near Tuolumne Meadows, September 9, 1869

Weariness rested away and I feel eager and ready for another excursion a month or two long in the same wonderful wilderness. Now, however, I must turn toward the lowlands, praying and hoping Heaven will shove me back again. . . . Comprehended in general views, the features of the wildest landscape seem to be as harmoniously related as the features of a human face. Indeed, they look human and radiate spiritual beauty, divine thought, however covered and concealed by rock and snow.

Mr. Delaney has hardly had time to ask me how I enjoyed my trip, though he has facilitated and encouraged my plans all summer and declares I'll be famous someday, a kind guess that seems strange and incredible to a wandering wilderness-lover with never a thought or dream of fame while humbly trying to trace and learn and enjoy Nature's lessons.   —MFS, 341–42

Near Tuolumne Meadows, September 13, 1869

Camped this evening at Yosemite Creek, close to the stream, on a little sand flat near our old campground. The vegetation is already brown and yellow and dry; the creek almost dry also. . . . The basin of this famous Yosemite stream is extremely rocky—seems fairly to be paved with domes like a street with big cobblestones. I wonder if I shall ever be allowed to explore it. It draws me so strongly, I would make any sacrifice to try to read its lessons. I thank God for this glimpse of it. The charms of these mountains are beyond all common reason, unexplainable and mysterious as life itself.   —MFS, 346–47

Sierra foothills, September 22, 1869

Here ends my forever memorable first high Sierra excursion. I have crossed the range of light, surely the brightest and best of all the Lord has built; and rejoicing in his glory, I gladly, gratefully, hopefully pray I may see it again.   —MFS, 354

4

Sanctum Sanctorum
Yosemite (1870–1874)

Muir moved to Yosemite Valley in December 1869, deter-
mined to make it his home. He found work as a laborer in a
sawmill, built a cabin at the foot of Yosemite Falls, and settled
in to what would become a three-year immersion in the Sierra
wilderness. He explored the high country above Yosemite in
his free time, scouring the peaks and valleys for evidence of
glacial activity, seeking to get as "near to the heart of the
world" as he could.

The following letter was written after Jeanne Carr invited
Muir to use her Oakland home as a place to "stay and refit" for
new explorations.

La Grange, California, November 15, 1869
Letter to Jeanne Carr

I thank you most heartily for the very kind invitation you sent
me. I could enjoy a blink of rest in your new home with a relish
that only those can know who have suffered solitary banish-
ment for so many years, but I must return to the mountains,
to Yosemite. I am told that the winter storms there will not be
easily borne, but I am bewitched, enchanted, and tomorrow I
must start for the great temple to listen to the winter songs and
sermons preached and sung only there.

Yosemite Valley, July 29, 1870
Letter to Jeanne Carr

I am very, very blessed. The Valley is full of people, but they do not annoy me. I revolve in pathless places in higher rocks than *the world* and his ribbony wife can reach. Had I not been blunted by hard work in the mill, and crazed by Sabbath raids among the high places of this heaven, I would have written you long since. I have spent every Sabbath for the last two months in the spirit world, screaming among the peaks and outside meadows like a negro Methodist in revival time, and every intervening clump of weekdays in trying to fix down and assimilate my shapeless harvests of revealed glory into the spirit and into the common earth of my existence; and I am rich, rich beyond measure, not in rectangular blocks of sifted knowledge, or in thin sheets of beauty hung picture-like about "the walls of memory," but in unselected atmospheres of terrestrial glory diffused evenly throughout my whole substance.

. . . and am just beginning to know how fully congenial you are. Would that you could share my mountain enjoyments! In all my wanderings through Nature's beauty, whether it is among the ferns at my cabin door, or in the high meadows and peaks, amid the spray and music of waterfalls, you are the first to meet me, and I often speak to you as verily present in the flesh.

Last Sabbath I was baptized in the irised foam of the Vernal [falls], and in the divine snow of Nevada [falls], and you were there also and stood in real presence by the sheet of joyous rapids below the bridge.   —KRS, 114

Yosemite Valley, Autumn 1870
Letter to Jeanne Carr

Some time ago I left all for Sequoia [Mariposa Grove today] and have been and am at his feet; fasting and praying for light, for is he not the greatest light in the woods, in the world? Where are such columns of sunshine, tangible, accessible, terrestrialized?

Well may I fast, not from bread, but from business, book-making, duty-going, and other trifles, and great is my reward already for the manly, treely sacrifice. . . . But I'm in the woods, woods, woods, and they are in *me-ee-ee*. The King tree and I have sworn eternal love—sworn it without swearing, and I have taken the sacrament with Douglas squirrel, drank Sequoia wine, Sequoia blood, and with its rosy purple drops I am writing this woody gospel letter. —KRS, 119–20

Yosemite Valley, June 4, 1871
Letter to Daniel Muir

Some time ago I rec'd a letter from you in which you requested a loan of a few dollars etc. [to begin a medical practice]. . . . I answered at once saying I would willingly send you what you wanted if I could get out of the valley in the fall to send it . . . perhaps you have not rec'd it. As long as I have a dollar you are far more than welcome to it. . . . I am in the heart of the mountains or I would send you $200 at once. . . . You shall never know a want that I can relieve wherever I may roam. . . .

I am working hard in every way but enjoy most of the work. Sometimes operating the sawmill, sometimes guiding in the mtns. I am more and more interested in science and am making many friends among the learned and the good who all seem to hail me as a brother.

I have no fixed practical aim, but am living in constant communion with Nature and follow my instincts and am most intensely happy.

Some day you will also behold the Lord's Yosemite. . . .[59]

Yosemite Valley, Date Unknown, 1871
Autobiographical Fragment

There are eight members in our family . . . all exemplary, stable, anti-revolutionary. Surely then, thought I, one may be spared for so fine an experiment [exploring the wilderness]. . . .

The remnants of compunction—the struggle concerning the serious business of settling down—gradually wasted and melted [away], and at length left me wholly free—born again!

I will follow my instincts, be myself for good or ill, and see what will be the upshot. As long as I live, I'll hear waterfalls and birds and winds sing. I'll interpret the rocks, learn the language of flood, storm, and the avalanche. I'll acquaint myself with the glaciers and wild gardens, and get as near the heart of the world as I can.

Hunger and cold, getting a living, hard work, poverty, loneliness, need of remuneration, giving up all thought of being known, getting married, etc., made no difference.[60]

Yosemite Valley, Spring 1871
Letter to Jeanne Carr

"The Spirit" has again led me into the wilderness, in opposition to all counter attractions, and I am once more in the glory of Yosemite.   —KRS, 133

The following letter was written from Fern Ledge, a narrow granite shelf next to upper Yosemite Falls, a few hundred feet above the Valley floor where Muir had planned to spend the night "in prayer." While walking behind the falls to observe the full moon through the mist, and in something of a "trance," he was struck by the falling water and almost fell to his death. He recovered and entered a state of higher consciousness where, he wrote, every "bolt and spray feels the hand of God." Though wet and chilled, he remained on the ledge, calming himself long enough to describe the experience to Mrs. Carr, whose presence he had felt from the beginning.

Yosemite Valley, April 3, 1871
Letter to Jeanne Carr

O, Mrs. Carr, that you could be here to mingle in this night-moon glory! I am in the upper Yosemite Falls and can hardly calm to write, but from my first baptism hours ago, you have been so present that I must try to fix you a written thought.

In the afternoon I came up the mountain here with a blanket and a piece of bread to spend the night in prayer among the spouts of this fall. But what can I say more than wish again that you might expose your soul to the rays of this heaven?

Silver from the moon illumines this glorious creation which we term "falls," and has laid a magnificent double prismatic bow at its base. . . . And every atom of the magnificent being from the thin silvery crest that does not dim the stars, to the inner arrowy, hardened shafts that strike onward like thunderbolts in sound and energy, all is life and spirit: every bolt and spray feels the hand of God. Oh, the music that is blessing me now! The sun of last week has given the grandest notes of all the yearly anthem.

I said that I was going to stop here until morning and pray a whole blessed night with the falls and the moon, but I am too wet and must go down. An hour or two ago I went out somehow on a little seam that extends along the wall behind the falls. I suppose I was in a trance, but I can positively say that I was in the body, for it is sorely battered and wetted. As I was gazing past the thin edge of the fall and away beneath the column to the brow of the rock, some heavy splashes of water struck me, driven hard against the wall. Suddenly I was darkened; down came a section of the outside tissue composed of spent comets. I crouched low, holding my breath, and anchored to some angular flakes of rock, took my baptism with moderately good faith.

When I dared to look up after the swaying column admitted light, I pounced behind a piece of ice which was wedged tight in the wall, and I no longer feared being washed off, and steady moonbeams slanting past the arching meteors gave me confidence to escape to this snug place where McChesney [J. B. McChesney, a mutual friend] and I slept one night, where I have a fire to dry my socks. This rock shelf, extending behind the falls, is about five hundred feet above the base of the fall on the perpendicular rock face.

How little do we know of ourselves, of our profoundest attractions and repulsions, of our spiritual affinities! How interesting does man become considered in his relations to the spirit of this rock and water! How significant does every atom of our world become amid the influences of those beings unseen, spiritual, angelic mountaineers that so throng these pure mansions of crystal foam and purple granite. . . .

Well, I must go down. I am disregarding all of the doctors' physiology in sitting here in this universal moisture. Farewell to you, and to all the beings about us. I shall have a glorious walk down the mountain in this thin white light, over the open brows grayed with Selaginella and through the thick black shadow caves in the live oaks, all stuck full of snowy lances of moonlight.

—KRS, 135–37

The following is excerpted from an article published in 1873 as "Explorations in the Great Tuolumne Canyon," based on Muir's journal entries at the time. That Muir descended into the three-thousand-foot canyon, followed the Tuolumne River for three miles, than climbed back out in the same day is a marvel. More intriguing though, are the glimpses he gives of the "doubleness" of his life in the wilderness, episodes when his "soul sets forth on rambles of its own" while his body remains "out of sight and forgotten. "It is a rare moment of spiritual transparency for the normally reticent Muir, who usually edited his more intimate personal observations out of his published writings.

Tuolumne Canyon, September 1871

This was my method of study: I drifted about from rock to rock, from stream to stream, from grove to grove. Where night found me, there I camped. When I discovered a new plant, I sat down beside it for a minute or day, to make its acquaintance and try to hear what it had to say. . . . I asked the boulders I met, whence they came and whither they were going. . . . It is astonishing how high and far we can climb mountains that we love, and how little we require food and clothing. . . .

No sane man in the hands of nature can doubt the doubleness of his life. Soul and body receive separate nourishment and separate exercise, and speedily reach a stage of development, wherein each is easily known apart from the other. Living artificially, we seldom see much of our real selves. Our torpid souls are hopelessly entangled with our torpid bodies, and not only is there a confused mingling of our own souls with our own bodies, but we hardly possess a separate existence from our neighbors.

The life of the mountaineer seems to be particularly favorable to the development of soul life, as well as limb life, each receiving abundance of exercise and abundance of food. We little suspect the capacity that even our flesh has for knowledge. Oftentimes in climbing canyon walls, I come to polished slopes that seem to be too steep to venture on. After scrutinizing them, carefully noting every dent and scratch that might give hope for foothold, I have decided they were unsafe. Yet my limbs, as if possessing a separate sense, would be of a different opinion and cross the condemned slopes against the remonstrances of the will. My legs sometimes transported me to camp, in the darkness, over cliffs and through bogs and forests that seem inaccessible to civilized legs in the daylight.

In like manner the soul sets forth at times upon rambles of its own. Our bodies, though meanwhile out of sight and forgotten, blend into the rest of nature, blind to the boundaries of individuals. But it is after both the body and soul of the mountaineer have worked hard, and enjoyed hard, that they are most palpably separate. Our weary limbs, lying at rest on the pine needles, make no attempt to follow after or sympathize with the nimble spirit that, apparently glad of the opportunity, wanders alone down gorges, along the beetling cliffs, or away among the peaks

and glaciers of the farthest landscapes, or into realms that eye
has not seen, nor ear heard; and when at length, we are ready
to return home to our flesh and bone tabernacle, we scarcely for
a moment or two know in what direction to seek for it. I have
often been unable to make my muscles move at such times, as if
the nerves concerned were broken, a state of things which, right
or wrong, would probably be explained by want of food and
extreme bodily exhaustion.   —JOM, 69–78

Mt. Clark Glacier, October 8 (?), 1871

Morning light rayless, beamless, unbodied of all its purple and
gold. No outgushing of solar glory pouring in torrents among
mountain peaks, baptizing them; but each pervaded with the
soul of light, boundless, tideless, newborn from the sun ere it has
received a hint of the good or bad from our star. . . . The trees,
the mountains are not near or far; they are made one, unseparate, unclothed, open to the divine soul, dissolved in the mysterious incomparable spirit of holy light! . . . They seem to wait only
in the very special presence of the great soul!   —JOM, 81–82

*While exploring the high country east of Yosemite Valley, Muir
was caught in a snowstorm and spent a day and night camped
in the lee of a large boulder on the shore of Lake Nevada [today,
Washburn Lake]. Around midnight, the sky cleared and Muir
found himself transported by a scene of such starlit clarity that
the mountains, lake, and trees appeared transparent, a single
"soul" lighted from within, "made wholly Godful." It is interesting to note that as the epiphany fades and Muir returns to
his senses, he finds that the lake too has "come back to earth."*[61]

Lake Nevada [Washburn Lake], October, 1871

Nearby a clump of tall pines at bend of lake shuts off all the
distant mountain, leaving nothing but the clear, present, living, soul-awakening purity of heaven. . . . The glacier-polish of

rounded brows brighter than any mirror, like windows of a house shining with light from the throne of God—to the very top [of the peaks] a pure vision in terrestrial beauty. . . . It is as if the lake, mountain, and trees had souls and formed one soul, which had died [in the storm] and gone before the throne of God, the great First Soul, and by direct, creative act of God had all earthly purity deepened, refined, brightness brightened, spirituality spiritualized, countenance, gestures made wholly Godful!

Not a cloud-memory in the sky. Not a ripple-memory on the lake, as if so complete in immortality that the very lake pulse were no longer needed, as if only the spiritual part of landscape life were left. I spring to my feet crying: "Heaven and earth! Rock is not light, not heavy, but is transparent and unfathomable as the sky itself. Every pore gushes, glows like a thought with immortal life. . . ."

Suddenly I hear the solemn wind-voices in the pines above me. All reflection is ruffled from the lake. It regains its voice of water lapping and tinkling on the sand. Stars leap from its waves and ripples. Lake Nevada has come back to earth with its own natural beauty, shored and mountained in terrestrial grandeur, wearing the jeweled garments of a winter storm!

—JOM, 83–84

Yosemite Valley, October (?), 1871
Letter to Jeanne Carr

I have been exploring the upper tributaries of the Cascade and Tamarak streams. And in particular all of the basin of the Yosemite Creek. . . . I fully believe that future investigation will show that, in the earlier ages of Sierra Nevada ice, vast glaciers flowed to the foot of the range east of Yosemite and also north and south at an elevation of nine thousand feet. . . . I have been living in these mountains in so haunting, soaring, floating a way that it seems strange to cast any kind of an anchor. All is so equal in glory, so ocean-like, that to choose one place above another is like drawing dividing lines in the sky.   —KRS, 150–51

Yosemite Valley, March 16, 1872
Letter to Jeanne Carr

I had a letter from Emerson the other day of which I told you
in another letter. He prophesies in the same dialect that you
are accustomed to use, that I shall one day go to the Atlantic
Coast. . . . I am glad to know by you and Emerson and others
living and dead that my unconditional surrender to Nature has
produced exactly what you have foreseen—that drifting without
human charts through light and dark, calm and storm I have
come to so glorious an ocean.   —KRS, 173

Yosemite Valley, (?) 1872
Letter to Therese Yelverton

Climb the mountains and get their good tidings. Nature's peace
will flow into you as sunshine flows into trees. The winds will
blow their own freshness into you, and the storms their energy,
while cares will drop off like autumn leaves.[62]

*Catharine Merrill became Muir's motherly confidant during his
time in Indianapolis. The second woman in the United States to
receive a doctorate, she taught English at Butler College and, in
a letter, was critical of Muir's decision to remain in the Yosemite
wilderness, apart from society. Below is Muir's response.*

Yosemite Valley, June 9, 1872
Letter to Catharine Merrill

I wish you could come here and rest a year in the simple unmin-
gled love fountains of God. You would then return to your
scholars with fresh truth gathered and absorbed from pines
and waters and deep singing winds, and you would find that
they all sang of fountain Love just as did Jesus Christ and all
of pure God manifest in whatever form. You say that good
men are "nearer to the heart of God than are woods and fields,

rocks and waters" Such distinctions and measurements seem strange to me. Rocks and waters, etc., are words of God and so are men. We all flow from one fountain Soul. All are expressions of one Love. God does not appear, and flow out, only from narrow chinks and round bored wells here and there in favored races and places, but He flows in grand undivided currents, shoreless and boundless over creeds and forms and all kinds of civilizations and peoples and beasts, saturating all and fountaining all.[63]

Yosemite Valley, August 28, 1872
Letter to Jeanne Carr

My horse and bread, etc., are ready for upward. . . . This time I go to the Merced group, one of whose mountains shelters a glacier. I will go over all the lakes and moraines, etc., there. Will be gone a week or two or so. . . .

Ink cannot tell the glow that lights me at this moment in turning to the mountains. I feel strong [enough] to leap Yosemite walls at a bound. Hotels and human impurity will be far below. I will fuse in spirit skies. I will touch naked God.

Farewell, or come meet in ghost between Red Mountain and Black on the star-sparkled ice.   —KRS, 188–89

Yosemite Valley, September 27, 1872
Letter to Ann G. Muir

Dear Mother,

I am just arrived from a long excursion up the great Tuolumne Canyon above Hetch Hetchy Valley. . . . I am able to do a great deal of very hard mountain exploration and someday will, if I live, tell you how mountains and river canyons and lake basins and meadows are made.

My life work is now before me plain enough, and it is full of hard labor and abundant in all kinds of pure reward.

Nature-God asks much and gives much and if we only are pure in heart we will see him in all times and in all lands. . . .[64]

The following is a much-cited passage where Muir found himself clinging to the face of a high peak, unable to move forward or retreat to safety. About to fall to his death, Muir was seized by a "preternatural" clarity which "assumed control" and allowed him to effortlessly climb to the top of the rock face. The passage is excerpted from an essay "A Near View of the High Sierra," which appears in chapter 8.

Mt. Ritter, Central Sierras, October 1872

At length, after attaining an elevation of about 12,800 feet, I found myself at the foot of a sheer drop in the bed of the avalanche channel I was tracing, which seemed absolutely to bar further progress. . . . The tried dangers beneath seemed even greater than that of the cliff in front; therefore, after scanning its face again and again, I began to scale it, picking my holds with intense caution. After gaining a point about halfway to the top, I was suddenly brought to a dead stop, with arms outspread, clinging close to the face of the rock, unable to move hand or foot either up or down. My doom appeared fixed. I *must* fall. There would be a moment of bewilderment, and then a lifeless rumble down the one general precipice to the glacier below.

When this final danger flashed upon me, I became nerve-shaken for the first time since setting foot on the mountains, and my mind seemed to fill with a stifling smoke. But this terrible eclipse lasted only a moment, when life blazed forth again with preternatural clearness. I seemed suddenly to become possessed of a new sense. The other self, bygone experiences, Instinct, or Guardian Angel—call it what you will—came forward and assumed control. Then my trembling muscles became firm again, every rift and flaw in the rock was seen as through a microscope, and my limbs moved with a positiveness and precision with which I seemed to have nothing at all to do. Had I been borne aloft upon wings, my deliverance could not have been more complete. —MC, 64–65

Yosemite Valley, December 30, 1872
Letter to Kate N. Daggett

I suppose our dear Mrs. Carr has told you of the eclipse of my life, years ago when my eyes were quenched just at the spring-dawn of summer when the voice of the bluebird began to appear mingled with the first flower-words of Erigenia and Anemone. But though in that terrible darkness I died to light, I lived again, and God who is Light has led me tenderly from light to light to the shoreless ocean of rayless beamless Spirit Light that bathes these holy mountains.[65]

The following passage is excerpted from a letter Muir wrote to Jeanne Carr upon his return to Yosemite after several weeks in Oakland during which he wrote his first series of articles for publication. Feeling "tainted" by the violent, materialistic culture of the 1870s Bay Area, Muir fled to Yosemite and climbed into the rugged Tenaya Canyon to fast and pray, passing the December night on a granite boulder without a blanket. The full letter, published as "A Geologist's Winter Walk," appears as chapter 7 in this volume.[66]

Yosemite Valley, December 25, 1872
Letter to Jeanne Carr

When I reached Yosemite, all the rocks seemed talkative, and more telling and lovable than ever. They are dear friends, and seemed to have warm blood gushing through their granite flesh; and I love them with a love intensified by long and close companionship. After I had bathed in the bright river, sauntered over the meadows, conversed with the domes, and played with the pines, I still felt blurred and weary, as if tainted in some way with the sticky sky of your streets. I determined, therefore, to run out for a while to say my prayers in the higher mountain temples. "The days are sunful," I said, "and, though now winter, no great danger need be encountered, and no sudden storm will block my return, if I am watchful."

The morning after this decision, I started up the canyon of Tenaya, caring little about the quantity of bread I carried; for, I thought, a fast and a storm and a difficult canyon were just the medicine I needed. When I passed Mirror Lake, I scarcely noticed it, for I was absorbed in the great Tissiack [Half Dome]—her crown a mile away in the hushed azure; . . .

This canyon is accessible only to mountaineers, and I was anxious to carry my barometer and clinometer through it to obtain sections and altitudes, so I chose it as the most attractive highway. [I was] ascending a precipitous rock front, smoothed by glacial action, when I suddenly fell — for the first time since I touched foot to Sierra rocks. After several somersaults, I became insensible from the shock, and when consciousness returned I found myself wedged among short, stiff bushes, trembling as if cold, not injured in the slightest.

Judging by the sun, I could not have been insensible very long; probably not a minute, possibly an hour; and I could not remember what made me fall, or where I had fallen from; but I saw that if I had rolled a little further, my mountain climbing would have been finished, for just beyond the bushes the canyon wall steepened and I might have fallen to the bottom. "There," said I, addressing my feet, to whose separate skill I had learned to trust night and day on any mountain, "that is what you get by intercourse with stupid town stairs and dead pavements." I felt degraded and worthless. I had not yet reached the most difficult portion of the canyon, but I determined to guide my humbled body over the most nerve-trying places I could find; for I was now awake and felt confident that the last of the town fog had been shaken from both head and feet. . . .

The moon is looking down into the canyon, and how marvelously the great rocks kindle to her light! Every dome, and brow, and swelling boss touched by her white rays, glows as if lighted with snow. I am now only a mile from last night's camp; and have been climbing and sketching all day in this difficult but instructive gorge. . . . How wholly infused with God is this one big word of love that we call the world! Good-night. Do you see the fire-glow on my ice-smoothed slab, and on my two ferns and the rubus and grass panicles? And do you hear how sweet a sleepsong the fall and cascades are singing?   —ST, 12–17

The Sierras, 1872 (?), Undated journal fragment

Mountains holy as Sinai. No mountains I know of are so alluring. None so hospitable, kindly, tenderly inspiring. It seems strange that everybody does not come at their call. They are given, like the gospel, without money and without price. "His heaven alone that is given away."

Here is calm so deep, grasses cease waving. . . . Wonderful, how completely everything in wild nature fits into us, as if truly part and parent of us. The sun shines not on us but in us. The rivers flow not past, but through us, thrilling, tingling, vibrating every fiber and cell of the substance of our bodies, making them glide and sing. The trees wave and the flowers bloom in our bodies as well as our souls, and every bird song, windsong, and tremendous storm song of the rocks in the heart of the mountains is our solemn, our very own, and sings our love.

The Sierras, 1872(?), Undated journal fragment

It is in these garden dells and glades, in peaceful spots where the winds are quiet, holding their breath, and every lily is motionless on its stem, that one is wholly free to enjoy self-forgetting. Here is no care, no time, and one seems to float in the deep, balmy summer tired after being thoroughly awakened and exhilarated by the dangers and enjoyments of some grand excursion into the thin deeps of the sky among the peaks.   —JOM, 170

The Sierras, 1872 (?) Undated journal fragment

Earth hath no sorrows that Earth cannot heal, or heaven cannot heal, for the Earth as seen in the clean wilds of the mountains is about as divine as anything the heart of man can conceive!

—JOM, 99

December 18, 1872
Letter to Asa Gray

I witnessed one of the most glorious of our mountain sunsets; not one of the assembled mountains seemed remote—all had ceased their labor of beauty and gathered around their parent sun to receive the evening blessing, and waiting angels could not be more solemnly hushed. The sun himself seemed to have reached a higher life as if he had died and only his soul were glowing with rayless, bodiless *Light*, and as Christ to his disciples, so this departing sun soul said to every precious beast, to every pine and weed, to every stream and mountain, "My peace I give unto you."[67]

Yosemite Valley, February 16, 1873

Every purely natural object is a conductor of divinity, and we have but to expose ourselves in a clean condition to any of these conductors to be fed and nourished by them. Only in this way can we procure our daily spirit bread. Only thus may we be filled with the Holy Ghost.   —JOM, 118

Yosemite Valley, March 12, 1873

All terrestrial things are essentially celestial, just as water beaten into foam, crystallized in ice, or warmed into vapor, or steam, dew or rain, is still water. Light is dashed upon the earth and changed in appearance just as water is dashed into spray. All human love is in like manner divine love.   —JOM, 130

Yosemite Valley, March 15, 1873

What is "higher," what is "lower" in nature? We speak of higher forms, higher types, etc., in the fields of scientific inquiry. Now all of the individual "things" or "beings" into which the world is wrought are sparks of the Divine Soul variously clothed upon with flesh, leaves, or that harder tissue called rock, water, etc.

Now we observe that in cold mountain altitudes, Spirit is but thinly and plainly clothed. . . . All of these varied forms, high and low, are simply portions of God, reheated from Him as a sun, and made terrestrial by the clothes they wear, and by the modifications of a corresponding kind in the God essence itself.
—JOM, 137–38

Yosemite Valley, March 30, 1873
Letter to Jeanne Carr

Oftentimes when I am free in the wilds I discover some rare beauty in lake, or cataract or mountain form and instantly seek to sketch it with my pencil, but the drawing is always enormously unlike the reality. So also in word sketches of the same beauties that are so living, so loving, so filled with warm God, there is the same infinite shortcoming. The few hard words make but a skeleton, fleshless, heartless, and when you read, the dead, bony words rattle in one's teeth. Yet I will not the less endeavor to do my poor best, believing that even these dead bone heaps called articles will occasionally contain hints to some living souls who know how to find them.   —KRS, 215

April 1873

The following is excerpted from an article Muir published in the Overland Monthly, *"Yosemite Valley in Flood."*

During the whole two days of the storm, no idle, unconscious water appeared, and the clouds, and winds, and rocks were inspired with corresponding activity and life. . . . The Merced [River], in some places, overflows its banks, having risen at once from a shallow, prattling, ill-proportioned stream, to a deep, majestic river. The upper Yosemite [Falls] is in full, gushing, throbbing glory of prime; still louder spring its shafts of song; still deeper grows the intense whiteness of its mingled meteors. . . . So sings Yosemite, with her hundred fellow-falls, to the trembling bushes, and solemn-waving pines, and winds, and clouds, and living, pulsing rocks—one stupendous unit of mountain power—one harmonious storm of mountain love.

On the third day the storm ceased. Frost killed the new falls; the clouds are withered and empty; a score of light is drawn across the sky, and our chapter of flood is finished. Visions like these do not remain with us as mere maps and pictures—flat shadows cast upon our minds, too bright, at times, when touched by association or will, to fade again from our view, like landscapes in the gloaming. They saturate every fiber of the body and soul, dwelling in us and with us, like holy spirits, through all of our after-deaths and after-lives.[68]

High Sierras, August 1873

Linnaeus says Nature never leaps, which means that God never shouts or spouts or speaks incoherently. The rocks and sublime canyons, and waters and winds, and all life structures—animals and ouzels, meadows and groves, and all the silver stars—are words of God, and they flow smooth and ripe from His lips.

—JOM, 153–54

Yosemite Valley, 1873, undated fragment

No wilderness in the world is so desolate as to be without divine ministers. God's love covers all the earth as the sky covers it and also fills it in every pore, and this love has voices heard by all who have ears to hear. Everything breaks into love just as in the spring banks of snow burst forth in loud rejoicing streams.⁶⁹

In September 1874, after spending ten months in Oakland producing a series of articles for publication—his first extended period away from the wilderness since 1867—Muir fled to Yosemite to recover his health and spirits. Upon reaching the Valley, he found that his immersion in city life had once again dimmed his spiritual sensibilities—neither the rocks nor the mountains seemed to "call" him. Muir concludes that the "Merced and Tuolumne" chapter of his life—the years of his "first summer," and the three years he lived in Yosemite—has concluded. Four months later, he will move permanently to the Bay Area to write. The following selection is excerpted from a letter to Jeanne Carr describing his journey back to the Yosemite after the long sojourn in Oakland.

Yosemite Valley, September 1874
Letter to Jeanne Carr

In the evening Black [Muir's companion] and I rode together up into the sugar pine forests and on to his old ranch in the moonlight. The grand priest-like pines held their arms above us in blessing. The wind sang songs of welcome. The cool glaciers and the running crystal fountains were in it. I was no longer on, but in the mountains—home again and my pulses were filled. . . .

The rush and gurgle and prolonged Aaaaaah of the stream coming up, sifting into the wind, was very solemnly impressive. It was here that you first seemed to join me. I reached up as Browny [Muir's horse] carried me underneath a big Douglas spruce and plucked one of its long plumy sprays, which brought you from the Oakland dead in a moment. You are more spruce then pine, though I never definitely knew it till now. . . .

Miles and miles of tree scripture along the sky, a Bible that will one day be read! The beauty of its letters and sentences have

burned me like fire through all these Sierra seasons. Yet I cannot
interpret their hidden thoughts. . . .

Few nights of my mountain life have been more eventful than
that of my ride in the woods from Coulterville, where I made my
reunion with the winds and pines. . . .

How cool and vital and recreative was the hale young mountain air. On higher, higher up into the holy of holies of the woods!
Pure white lustrous clouds overshadowed the massive congrega-
tions of silver fir and pine. We entered, and a thousand living
arms were waved in solemn blessing. An infinity of mountain
life. How complete is the absorption of one's life into the spirit
of mountain woods. . . .

 A deep canyon filled with blue air now comes in view on the
right. That is the Valley of the Merced [River], and the highest
rocks visible through the trees belong to the Yosemite Valley.
More miles of glorious forest, then out into free light and down,
down, down into the groves and meadows of Yosemite. Sierra
sculpture in its entirety without the same study on the spot. No
one of the rocks seems to call me now, nor any of the distant
mountains. Surely this Merced and Tuolumne chapter of my life
is done.   —LL, 2:21–26

Yosemite Valley, October 7, 1874
Letter to Jeanne Carr

I expected to be among the foothill drift long ago, but the mountains fairly seized me, and, ere I knew, I was up the Merced canyon, where we were last year, past Shadow [Washburn] and
Merced lakes and our soda springs, etc. I returned last night. Had
a glorious storm and a thousand sacred beauties that seemed yet
more and more divine. I . . . was in a kind of calm, uncurable
ecstasy. I am hopelessly and forever a mountaineer. . . . Civilization and fever and all the morbidness that has been hooted at
me has not dimmed my glacial eyes, and I care to live only to
entice people to look at Nature's loveliness. My own special self
is nothing.   —KRS, 252–53

5

Voice of the Wilderness
The World (1875–1913)

Muir's spiritual reflections decreased substantially as he settled into a career as a nature writer and journalist in the 1870s. He married in 1880, managed the Martinez farm through the decade, and then led the conservation battles of the 1890s. Nonetheless, especially during his Alaska travels, Muir produced occasional passages whose spiritual intensity and lyrical beauty rival the finest of his Yosemite reflections.

In July 1879 Muir traveled to Alaska on the first of several expeditions. He hoped to observe how glaciation shaped the landscape and altered plant, animal, and human habitats in an extreme environment. Alaska would become for Muir a favorite refuge, the one remaining untamed wilderness on the North American continent.

Mt. Shasta, April 1875

At the summit [of Mt. Shasta], the sky was of the thinnest purest azure; spiritual life filled every pore of rock and cloud; and we reveled in the marvelous abundance and beauty of the landscapes by which we were encircled.[70]

San Joaquin River, August 1875

Morning comes again, hallowed with all the deeds of night. Here it is six or seven thousand feet above the sea, yet in all this tranquil scene we feel no remoteness, no rest from care and chafing

duties because here they have no existence. Every sense is satisfied. For us there is no past, no future. We live in the present and
are full. No room for hungry hopes, none for regrets, none for
exultation, none for fear.   —JOM, 214

Alaska, July 1879

As I lingered, gazing on the vast show, luminous, shadowy clouds
seemed to increase in glory of color and motion, now fondling
the highest peaks with infinite tenderness of touch, now hover-
ing above them like eagles over their nests.

When night was drawing near, I ran down the flowery slopes
exhilarated, thanking God for the gift of this great day. The
setting sun fired the clouds. All the world seemed newborn.
Everything, even the commonest, was seen in new light and was
looked at with new interest as if never seen before. The plant
people seemed glad, as if rejoicing with me, the little ones as
well as the trees, while every feature of the peak and its traveled
boulders seemed to know what I had been about and the depth
of my joy, as if they could read faces.   —TA, 96

Alaska, July 1879

In the evening, after witnessing the unveiling of the majestic
peaks and glaciers and their baptism in the down-pouring sunbeams, it seemed inconceivable that nature could have anything
finer to show us. Nevertheless, compared with what was to come
the next morning, all that was as nothing. . . .

The calm dawn gave no promise of anything uncommon. . . .
The sunrise we did not see at all, for we were beneath the shadows of the fjord cliffs; but in the midst of our studies, while
the Indians [Muir's guides] were getting ready to sail, we were
startled by the sudden appearance of a red light burning with
a strange, unearthly splendor on the topmost peak of the Fair-
weather Mountains. Instead of vanishing as suddenly as it had
appeared, it spread and spread until the whole range down to

the level of the glaciers was filled with the celestial fire. In color it was at first a vivid crimson, with a thick, furred appearance, as fine as the alpenglow, yet indescribably rich indeed. . . . Every mountain apparently was glowing from the heart like molten metal fresh from a furnace. Beneath the frosty shadows of the fjord we stood hushed and awe stricken, gazing at the holy vision; and had we seen the heavens opened and God made manifest, our attention could not have been more tremendously strained.

When the highest peak began to burn, it did not seem to be steeped in sunshine, however glorious, but rather as if it had been thrust into the body of the sun itself. Then the supernal fire slowly descended . . . until all the mighty host stood transfigured, hushed, and thoughtful, as if awaiting the coming of the Lord. The white, rayless light of morning, seen when I was alone amid the peaks of the California Sierra, had always seemed to me the most telling of all the terrestrial manifestations of God. But here the mountains themselves were made divine and declared his glory in terms still more impressive. How long we gazed I never knew. The glorious vision passed away in a gradual, fading change. . . . We turned and sailed away, joining the outgoing icebergs, while "Gloria in excelsis" still seemed to be sounding over all the white landscape, and our burning hearts were ready for any fate, feeling that, whatever the future might have in store, the treasures we had gained this glorious morning would enrich our lives forever.   —TA, 152–54

Martinez, California, June 16, 1885
Letter to Helen Hunt Jackson

When I came to California from the swamps of Florida, full of malarial poison, and I crawled up the mountains over the snow into the blessed woods about Yosemite Valley, the exquisite pleasure of convalescence and exuberant rebound to perfect health that came to me at once seems still as fresh and vivid after all these years as if enjoyed but yesterday. . . . But go to

the mountains where and how you will, you soon will be free
from the effects of this confusion, and God's sky will bend down
about you as if made for you alone, and the pines will spread
their healing arms above you and bless you and make you well
again.   —LL, 2:198–203

February 23, 1887
Letter to Janet Douglas Moores

Surely you must remember those holiday walks, and also you
coming into my dark room with light when I was blind! And
what light has filled me since that time, I am sure you will be
glad to know—the richest sun-gold flooding these California
valleys, the spiritual Alpine glow steeping the high peaks, silver
light on the sea, the white, glancing sun spangles on rivers and
lakes, light on the myriad stars of the snow, light sifting through
the angles of sun-beaten icebergs, light in glacier caves, irised
spray wafting from white waterfalls, and the light of calm starry
nights beheld from mountaintops dipping deep into the clear air.
Aye, my lassie, it is a blessed thing to go free in the light of this
beautiful world, to see God playing upon everything, as a man
would play on an instrument, His fingers upon the lightning and
torrent, and every wave of sea and sky, and every living thing,
making altogether sing and shine in sweet accord, the one love-
harmony of the universe.   —LL, 2:215–16

Alaska, June 1890

Not in these fields, God's wilds, will you ever hear this sad
moment of disappointment, "All is vanity" . . . Indeed, some of
the days I have spent alone in the depths of the wilderness have
shown me that immortal life beyond the grave is not essential to
perfect happiness, for these diverse days were so complete there
was no sense of time in them, they had no definite beginning or
ending, and formed a kind of terrestrial immortality.
                                                —JOM, 301

Alaska, June–July 1890

In God's wildness lies the hope of the world—the great, fresh, unblighted, unredeemed wilderness. The galling harness of civilization drops off, and the wounds heal ere we are aware.

—JOM, 317

Alaska, July 11, 1890

The clearest way into the universe is through a forest wilderness.

—JOM, 313

Alaska, July 1890

In the mountains, free, unimpeded, the imagination feeds on objects immense and eternal. Divine influences, however invisible, are showered down on us as thick as snowflakes in a snowstorm.

—JOM, 315

Alaska, July 13, 1890

I am often asked if I am not lonesome on my solitary excursions. It seems so self-evident that one cannot be lonesome where everything is wild and beautiful and busy and steeped with God, that the question is hard to answer—seems silly.

Every particle of rock or water or air has God by its side leading it the way it should go. How else would it know where to go or what to do?

—JOM, 319

Martinez, California, 1901

Thousands of tired, nerve-shaken, over-civilized people are beginning to find out that going to the mountains is going home; that wildness is a necessity; and that mountain parks and reservations are useful not only as fountains of timber and irrigating rivers, but as fountains of life.

—ONP, 1

Martinez, California, 1901

Benevolent, solemn, fateful, pervaded with divine light, every landscape glows like a countenance hallowed in eternal repose;

and every one of its living creatures, clad in flesh and leaves, and every crystal of its rocks, whether on the surface shining in the sun or buried miles deep in what we call darkness, is throbbing and pulsing with the heartbeats of God.   —ONP, 76

Martinez, California, 1901

To an observer upon this adamantine old monument [a granite boulder] in the midst of such scenery, getting glimpses of the thoughts of God, the day seems endless, the sun stands still. Much faithless fuss is made over the passage in the Bible telling of the standing still of the sun for Joshua. Here, you may learn that the miracle occurs for every devout mountaineer, for everybody doing anything worth doing, seeing anything worth seeing. One day is as a thousand years, a thousand years as one day, and while yet in the flesh, you enjoy immortality.   —ONP, 92

The Sierras, 1902?

[John Muir] threw up his hands in a grand gesture, "This is the morning of creation," he cried, "the whole thing is beginning now! The mountains are singing together."[71]

The Sierras, Unknown date

One day when Albert Palmer was resting along a Sierra trail, John Muir overtook him and began to chat. Palmer asked, "Mr. Muir, someone told me you did not approve of the word 'hike.' Is that so?" Muir replied, "I don't like either the word or the thing. People ought to 'saunter' in the mountains—not 'hike!' Do you know the origin of that word saunter? It's a beautiful word. Away back in the middle ages people used to go on pilgrimages to the Holy Land, and when people in the villages through which they passed asked where they were going, they would reply, *A la sainte terre*, 'To the Holy Land.' And so they became known as sainte-terrers or saunterers. Now these mountains are our Holy Land, and we ought to saunter through them reverently, not 'hike' through them."[72]

Martinez, California, 1913

All the merry dwellers of the trees and streams, and the myriad swarms of the air, called into life by the sunbeam of a summer morning, go home through death, wings folded perhaps in the last red rays of sunset of the day they were first tried. Trees towering in the sky, braving storms of centuries, flowers turning faces to the light for a single day or hour, having enjoyed their share of life's feast—all alike passed on and away under the law of death and love. Yet all are our brothers and they enjoy life as we do, share heaven's blessings with us, die and are buried in hallowed ground, come with us out of eternity and return into eternity. —JOM, 440

Martinez, California, Undated, 1913 (?)

This grand show is eternal. It is always sunrise somewhere; the dew is never all dried at once; the shower is forever falling; vapor is ever rising. Eternal sunrise, eternal sunset, eternal dawn and gloaming, on sea and continents and islands, each in its turn, as the round earth rolls. —JOM, 438

Martinez, California, Undated, 1913 (?)

Not like my taking the veil—no solemn abjuration of the world. I only went out for a walk, and finally concluded to stay out till sundown, for going out, I found, was really going in.
—JOM, 439

6

Twenty Hill Hollow

This is excerpted from an essay Muir wrote but never published about his first year living as a shepherd in California's Sierra foothills. As mentioned earlier, it was in Twenty Hill Hollow that Muir fully recovered from his malarial fever and experienced his first ecstatic responses to a sacred natural world. His official biographer, William Frederic Badè, included the essay at the end of his 1915 edition of Muir's Thousand-Mile Walk to the Gulf.[73]

Were we to cross-cut the Sierra Nevada into blocks a dozen miles or so in thickness, each section would contain a Yosemite Valley and a river, together with a bright array of lakes and meadows, rocks and forests. The grandeur and inexhaustible beauty of each block would be so vast and over-satisfying that to choose among them would be like selecting slices of bread cut from the same loaf. One bread-slice might have burnt spots, answering to craters; another would be more browned; another, more crusted or raggedly cut; but all essentially the same. In no greater degree would the Sierra slices differ in general character. Nevertheless, we all would choose the Merced River slice, because, being easier of access, it has been nibbled and tasted, and pronounced very good; and because of the concentrated form of its Yosemite, caused by certain conditions of baking, yeasting, and glacier-frosting of this portion of the great Sierra loaf. In like manner, we readily perceive that the great central plain is one batch of bread—one golden cake—and we are loath to leave these magnificent loaves for crumbs, however good.

After our smoky sky has been washed in the rains of winter, the whole complex row of Sierras appears from the plain as a simple wall, slightly beveled, and colored in horizontal bands laid one above another, as if entirely composed of partially straightened rainbows. So, also, the plain seen from the mountains has the same simplicity of smooth surface, colored purple and yellow, like a patchwork of irised clouds. But when we descend to this smooth-furred sheet, we discover complexity in its physical conditions equal to that of the mountains, though less strongly marked. In particular, that portion of the plain lying between the Merced River and the Tuolumne River, within ten miles of the slaty foothills, is most elaborately carved into valleys, hollows, and smooth undulations, and among them is laid the Merced Yosemite of the plain—Twenty Hill Hollow.

This delightful hollow is less than a mile in length, and of just sufficient width to form a well-proportioned oval. It is situated about midway between the two rivers, and five miles from the Sierra foothills. Its banks are formed of twenty hemispherical hills; hence its name. They surround and enclose it on all sides, leaving only one narrow opening toward the southwest for the escape of its waters. The bottom of the Hollow is about two hundred feet below the level of the surrounding plain, and the tops of its hills are slightly below the general level. Here is no towering dome, no Tissiack [Half Dome] to mark its place; and one may ramble close upon its rim before he is made aware of its existence. Its twenty hills are as wonderfully regular in size and position as in form. They are like big marbles half buried in the ground, each poised and settled daintily into its place at a regular distance from its fellows, making a charming fairy-land of hills, with small, grassy valleys between, each valley having a tiny stream of its own, which leaps and sparkles out into the open hollow, uniting to form Hollow Creek.

Like all others in the immediate neighborhood, these twenty hills are composed of stratified lavas mixed with mountain drift in varying proportions. Some strata are almost wholly made up of volcanic matter, lava and cinders—thoroughly ground and mixed by the waters that deposited them; others are largely composed of slate and quartz boulders of all degrees of coarseness, forming conglomerates. A few clear, open sections occur, exposing an elaborate history of seas, and glaciers, and volcanic floods—chapters of cinders and ashes that picture dark days when these bright snowy mountains were clouded in smoke and rivered and laked with living fire. A fearful age, say mortals, when these Sierras flowed lava to the sea. What horizons of flame! What atmospheres of ashes and smoke. . . .

Twenty Hill Hollow is a fine illustration of a valley created by erosion of water. Here are no Washington columns, no angular El Capitans. . . . The canyons, cut in soft lavas, are not so deep as to require a single earthquake at the hands of science, much less a baker's dozen of those convenient tools demanded for the making of mountain Yosemites, and our moderate arithmetical standards are not outraged by a single magnitude of this simple, comprehensible hollow. . . .

The Hollow is not rich in birds. The meadowlark homes there, and the little burrowing owl, the killdeer, and a species of sparrow. Occasionally a few ducks pay a visit to its waters, and a few tall herons—the blue and the white—may at times be seen stalking along the creek; and the sparrow hawk and gray eagle come to hunt. The lark, who does nearly all the singing for the Hollow, is not identical in species with the meadowlark of the East, though closely resembling it; richer flowers and skies have inspired him with a better song than was ever known to the Atlantic lark.

I have noted three distinct lark-songs here. The words of the first, which I committed to memory at one of their special meetings, spelled as sung, are, "Wee-ro spee-ro wee-o weer-ly wee-it."

On the 20th of January 1869, they sang "Queed-lix boodle,"
repeating it with great regularity, for hours together, to music
sweet as the sky that gave it. On the 22nd of the same month,
they sang "Chee chool cheedildy choodildy." An inspiration
is this song of the blessed lark, and universally absorbable by
human souls. . . . God be thanked for this blessed instrument hid
beneath the feathers of a lark.

The eagle does not dwell in the Hollow; he only floats there to
hunt the long-eared hare. One day I saw a fine specimen alight
upon a hillside. I was at first puzzled to know what power could
fetch the sky-king down into the grass with the larks. Watching
him attentively, I soon discovered the cause of his earthiness. He
was hungry and stood watching a long-eared hare, which stood
erect at the door of his burrow, staring his winged fellow mortal
full in the face. They were about ten feet apart. Should the eagle
attempt to snatch the hare, he would instantly disappear in the
ground. Should long-ears, tired of inaction, venture to skim the
hill to some neighboring burrow, the eagle would swoop above
him and strike him dead with a blow of his pinions, bear him to
some favorite rock table, satisfy his hunger, wipe off all marks of
grossness, and go again to the sky. . . .

All the seasons of the Hollow are warm and bright, and
flowers bloom through the whole year. But the grand com-
mencement of the annual genesis of plant and insect life is governed by the setting-in of the rains, in December or January.
The air, hot and opaque, is then washed and cooled. Plant seeds,
which for six months have lain on the ground dry as if gar-
nered in a farmer's bin, at once unfold their treasured life. Flies
hum their delicate tunes. Butterflies come from their coffins, like
cotyledons from their husks. The network of dry water-courses,
spread over valleys and hollows, suddenly gushes with bright
waters, sparkling and pouring from pool to pool, like dusty
mummies risen from the dead and set living and laughing with
color and blood. The weather grows in beauty, like a flower. Its

roots in the ground develop day-clusters a week or two in size, divided by and shaded in foliage of clouds; or round hours of ripe sunshine wave and spray in sky-shadows, like racemes of berries half hidden in leaves.

These months of so-called rainy season are not filled with rain. Nowhere else in North America, perhaps in the world, are Januarys so balmed and glowed with vital sunlight. Referring to my notes of 1868 and 1869, I find that the first heavy general rain of the season fell on the 18th of December. January yielded to the Hollow, during the day, only twenty hours of rain, which was divided among six rainy days. February had only three days on which rain fell, amounting to eighteen and one-half hours in all. March had five rainy days. April had three, yielding seven hours of rain. May also had three wet days, yielding nine hours of rain, and completed the so-called "rainy season" for that year, which is probably about an average one. It must be remembered that this rain record has nothing to do with what fell in the night.

The ordinary rainstorm of this region has little of that outward pomp and sublimity of structure so characteristic of the storms of the Mississippi Valley. Nevertheless, we have experienced rainstorms out on these treeless plains, in nights of solid darkness, as impressively sublime as the noblest storms of the mountains. . . . One magnificent storm from the northwest occurred on the 21st of March; an immense, round-browed cloud came sailing over the flowery hills in most imposing majesty, bestowing water as from a sea. The passionate rain-gush lasted only about one minute, but was nevertheless the most magnificent cataract of the sky mountains that I ever beheld. A portion of calm sky toward the Sierras was brushed with thin, white cloud-tissue, upon which the rain-torrent showed to a great height a cloud waterfall, which, like those of Yosemite, was neither spray, rain, nor solid water. . . .

At the end of January, four plants were in flower: a small white cress, growing in large patches; a low-set, umbeled plant, with yellow flowers; an eriogonum, with flowers in leafless spangles; and a small boragewort. Five or six mosses had adjusted their hoods and were in the prime of life. In February, squirrels, hares, and flowers were in springtime joy. Bright plant-constellations shone everywhere about the Hollow. Ants were getting ready for work, rubbing and sunning their limbs upon the husk-piles around their doors; fat, pollen-dusted, "burly, dozing bumble-bees" were rumbling among the flowers; and spiders were busy mending up old webs or weaving new ones. Flowers were born every day and came gushing from the ground like gayly dressed children from a church. The bright air became daily more songful with fly-wings, and sweeter with breath of plants. . . .

Toward the end of this month or the beginning of April, plant life is at its greatest height. Few have any just conception of its amazing richness. Count the flowers of any portion of these twenty hills, or of the bottom of the Hollow, among the streams: you will find that there are from one to ten thousand upon every square yard, counting the heads of *Compositae* as single flowers. Yellow *Compositae* form by far the greater portion of this goldy-way. Well may the sun feed them with his richest light, for these shining sunlets are his very children—rays of his ray, beams of his beam! One would fancy that these California days receive more gold from the ground than they give to it. The earth has indeed become a sky; and the two cloudless skies, raying toward each other flower-beams and sun-beams, are fused and congolded into one glowing heaven. By the end of April most of the Hollow plants have ripened their seeds and died; but, undecayed, still assist the landscape with color from persistent involucres and corolla-like heads of chaffy scales. . . .

The Hollow may easily be visited by tourists *en route* for Yosemite, as it is distant only about six miles from Snelling's

[Snelling today]. It is at all seasons interesting to the naturalist; but it has little that would interest the majority of tourists
earlier than January or later than April. If you wish to see how
much of light, life, and joy can be got into a January, go to this
blessed Hollow. If you wish to see a plant-resurrection—myriads of bright flowers crowding from the ground, like souls to
a judgment—go to Twenty Hills in February. If you are traveling for health, play truant to doctors and friends, fill your
pocket with biscuits, and hide in the hills of the Hollow, lave
in its waters, tan in its golds, bask in its flower-shine, and your
baptisms will make you a new creature indeed. Or, choked in
the sediments of society, so tired of the world, here will your
hard doubts disappear, your carnal incrustations melt off, and
your soul breathe deep and free in God's shoreless atmosphere
of beauty and love.

Never shall I forget my baptism in this font. It happened in
January, a resurrection day for many a plant and for me. I suddenly found myself on one of its hills; the Hollow overflowed
with light, as a fountain, and only small, sunless nooks were
kept for mosseries and ferneries. Hollow Creek spangled and
mazed like a river. The ground steamed with fragrance. Light,
of unspeakable richness, was brooding the flowers. Truly, said
I, is California the Golden State—in metallic gold, in sun gold,
and in plant gold. The sunshine for a whole summer seemed
condensed into the chambers of that one glowing day. Every
trace of dimness had been washed from the sky; the mountains
were dusted and wiped clean with clouds—Pacheco Peak and
Mt. Diablo, and the waved blue wall between; the grand Sierra
stood along the plain, colored in four horizontal bands:—the
lowest, rose purple; the next higher, dark purple; the next,
blue; and, above all, the white row of summits pointing to the
heavens.

It may be asked, What have mountains fifty or a hundred miles
away to do with Twenty Hill Hollow? To lovers of the wild, these

mountains are not a hundred miles away. Their spiritual power
and the goodness of the sky make them near, as a circle of friends.
They rise as a portion of the hilled walls of the Hollow. You
cannot feel yourself out of doors; plain sky and mountains ray
beauty which you feel. You bathe in these spirit-beams, turning
round and round, as if warming at a campfire. Presently you lose
consciousness of your own separate existence: you blend with the
landscape and become part and parcel of nature.

7

A Geologist's Winter Walk

This essay was originally a letter written to Jeanne Carr on Christmas Day 1872 from Yosemite Valley. It chronicles Muir's return to Yosemite after several weeks in Oakland during which he wrote his first series of articles for publication. Muir felt "tainted" by the violent, materialistic culture of the 1870s Bay Area and fled one day in December to Yosemite, sometimes running on foot. Certain that he had been spiritually polluted by the urban atmosphere, Muir imposed an ascetic discipline on himself, climbing into the rugged Tenaya Canyon at the east end of the Valley to fast and pray, taking only some bread scraps for food and passing the December night on a granite boulder without a blanket. Not written for publication, the essay reveals Muir's passion for nature and his abiding faith in its spiritually restorative powers.[74]

After reaching Turlock, I sped afoot over the stubble fields and through miles of brown hemizonia and purple erigeron, to Hopeton, conscious of little more than that the town was behind and beneath me, and the mountains above and before me; on through the oaks and chaparral of the foothills to Coulterville; and then ascended the first great mountain step upon which grows the sugar pine. Here I slackened pace, for I drank the spicy, resiny wind, and beneath the arms of this noble tree I felt that I was safely home. Never did pine trees seem so dear. How sweet was their breath and their song, and how grandly

117

they winnowed the sky! I tingled my fingers among their tassels and rustled my feet among their brown needles and burrs, and was exhilarated and joyful beyond all I can write.

When I reached Yosemite, all the rocks seemed talkative, and more telling and lovable than ever. They are dear friends and seemed to have warm blood gushing through their granite flesh; and I love them with a love intensified by long and close companionship. After I had bathed in the bright river, sauntered over the meadows, conversed with the domes, and played with the pines, I still felt blurred and weary, as if tainted in some way with the sky of your streets. I determined, therefore, to run out for a while to say my prayers in the higher mountain temples. "The days are sunful," I said, "and, though now winter, no great danger need be encountered, and no sudden storm will block my return, if I am watchful."

The morning after this decision, I started up the canyon of Tenaya, caring little about the quantity of bread I carried; for, I thought, a fast and a storm and a difficult canyon were just the medicine I needed. When I passed Mirror Lake, I scarcely noticed it, for I was absorbed in the great Tissiack—her crown a mile away in the hushed azure; her purple granite drapery flowing in soft and graceful folds down to my feet, embroidered gloriously around with deep, shadowy forest. I have gazed on Tissiack a thousand times—in days of solemn storms, and when her form shone divine with the jewelry of winter, or was veiled in living clouds; and I have heard her voice of winds, and snowy, tuneful waters when floods were falling; yet never did her soul reveal itself more impressively than now. I hung about her skirts, lingering timidly, until the higher mountains and glaciers compelled me to push up the canyon.

This canyon is accessible only to mountaineers, and I was anxious to carry my barometer and clinometer through it, to obtain sections and altitudes, so I chose it as the most attractive highway. After I had passed the tall groves that stretch a mile above

Mirror Lake, and scrambled around the Tenaya Fall, which is just at the head of the lake groves, I crept through the dense and spiny chaparral that plushes the roots of the mountains here for miles in warm green, and was ascending a precipitous rock front, smoothed by glacial action, when I suddenly fell—for the first time since I touched foot to Sierra rocks. After several somersaults, I became insensible from the shock, and when consciousness returned I found myself wedged among short, stiff bushes, trembling as if cold, not injured in the slightest.

Judging by the sun, I could not have been insensible very long; probably not a minute, possibly an hour; and I could not remember what made me fall, or where I had fallen from; but I saw that if I had rolled a little further, my mountain climbing would have been finished, for just beyond the bushes the canyon wall steepened and I might have fallen to the bottom. "There," said I, addressing my feet, to whose separate skill I had learned to trust night and day on any mountain, "that is what you get by intercourse with stupid town stairs, and dead pavements." I felt degraded and worthless. I had not yet reached the most difficult portion of the canyon, but I determined to guide my humbled body over the most nerve-trying places I could find; for I was now awake, and felt confident that the last of the town fog had been shaken from both head and feet.

I camped at the mouth of a narrow gorge which is cut into the bottom of the main canyon, determined to take earnest exercise next day. No plushy boughs did my ill-behaved bones enjoy that night, nor did my bumped head get a spicy cedar plume pillow mixed with flowers. I slept on a naked boulder, and when I awoke all my nervous trembling was gone.

The gorged portion of the canyon, in which I spent all the next day, is about a mile and a half in length; and I passed the time in tracing the action of the forces that determined this peculiar bottom gorge, which is an abrupt, ragged-walled, narrow-throated canyon, formed in the bottom of the wide-mouthed, smooth, and beveled main canyon. I will not stop now to tell you more; some day you may see it, like a shadowy line, from Cloud's Rest. In high water, the stream occupies all the bottom of the gorge, surging and chafing in glorious power from wall to wall. But the sound of the grinding was low as I entered the gorge, scarcely hoping to be able to pass through its entire length. By cool efforts, along glassy, ice-worn slopes, I reached the upper end in a little over a day, but was compelled to pass the second night in the gorge, and in the moonlight I wrote you this short pencil-letter in my notebook:

> The moon is looking down into the canyon, and how marvelously the great rocks kindle to her light! Every dome, and brow, and swelling boss touched by her white rays, glows as if lighted with snow. I am now only a mile from last night's camp and have been climbing and sketching all day in this difficult but instructive gorge. It is formed in the bottom of the main canyon, among the roots of Cloud's Rest. It begins at the filled-up lake basin where I camped last night and ends a few hundred yards above, in another basin of the same kind. The walls everywhere are craggy and vertical, and in some places they overlean. It is only from twenty to sixty feet wide, and not, though black and broken enough, the thin, crooked mouth of some mysterious abyss; but it was eroded, for in many places I saw its solid, seamless floor.

> I am sitting on a big stone, against which the stream divides, and goes brawling by in rapids on both sides; half of my rock is white in the light, half in shadow. As I look from the opening jaws of this shadowy gorge, South Dome is immediately in front—high in the stars, her face turned from the moon, with the rest of her body gloriously muffled in waved folds of granite. On the left, sculptured from the main Cloud's Rest ridge, are three

magnificent rocks, sisters of the great South Dome. On
the right is the massive, moonlit front of Mt. Watkins,
and between, low down in the furthest distance, is Senti-
nel Dome, girdled and darkened with forest. In the near
foreground Tenaya Creek is singing against boulders
that are white with snow and moonbeams. Now look
back twenty yards, and you will see a waterfall fair as
a spirit; the moonlight just touches it, bringing it into
relief against a dark background of shadow. A little to
the left, and a dozen steps this side of the fall, a flicker-
ing light marks my camp—and a precious camp it is.
A huge, glacier-polished slab, falling from the smooth,
glossy flank of Cloud's Rest, happened to settle on edge
against the wall of the gorge. I did not know that this
slab was glacier-polished until I lighted my fire. Judge of
my delight. I think it was sent here by an earthquake. It
is about twelve feet square. I wish I could take it home
for a hearthstone. Beneath this slab is the only place in
this torrent-swept gorge where I could find sand sufficient for a bed.

I expected to sleep on the boulders, for I spent most of the
afternoon on the slippery wall of the canyon, endeavor-
ing to get around this difficult part of the gorge, and was
compelled to hasten down here for water before dark. I
shall sleep soundly on this sand; half of it is mica. Here,
wonderful to behold, are a few green stems of prickly
rubus, and a tiny grass. They are here to meet us. Ay,
even here in this darksome gorge, "frightened and tor-
mented" with raging torrents and choking avalanches
of snow. . . . How wholly infused with God is this one
big word of love that we call the world! Good-night. Do
you see the fire-glow on my ice-smoothed slab, and on
my two ferns and the rubus and grass panicles? And do

you hear how sweet a sleep-song the fall and cascades
are singing?

The water-ground chips and knots that I found fastened
between the rocks kept my fire alive all through the night. Next
morning I rose nerved and ready for another day of sketching
and noting, and any form of climbing. I escaped from the gorge
about noon, after accomplishing some of the most delicate feats
of mountaineering I ever attempted; and here the canyon is all
broadly open again—the floor luxuriantly forested with pine,
and spruce, and silver fir, and brown-trunked libocedrus. The
walls rise in Yosemite forms, and Tenaya Creek comes down
seven hundred feet in a white brush of foam. This is a little
Yosemite valley. It is about two thousand feet above the level of
the main Yosemite and about twenty-four hundred below Lake
Tenaya.

I found the lake frozen, and the ice was so clear and unruffled
that the surrounding mountains and the groves that look down
upon it were reflected almost as perfectly as I ever beheld them
in the calm evening mirrors of summer. At a little distance, it was
difficult to believe the lake frozen at all; and when I walked out
on it, cautiously stamping at short intervals to test the strength
of the ice, I seemed to walk mysteriously, without adequate
faith, on the surface of the water. The ice was so transparent
that I could see through it the beautifully wave-rippled, sandy
bottom, and the scales of mica glinting back the down-pouring
light. When I knelt down with my face close to the ice, through
which the sunbeams were pouring, I was delighted to discover
myriads of Tyndall's six-rayed water flowers, magnificently
colored.

A grand old mountain mansion is this Tenaya region! In the
glacier period it was a mer de glace, far grander than the mer
de glace of Switzerland, which is only about half a mile broad.
The Tenaya mer de glace was not less than two miles broad,
late in the glacier epoch, when all the principal dividing crests

were bare; and its depth was not less than fifteen hundred feet. Ice streams from Mounts Lyell and Dana, and all the mountains between, and from the nearer Cathedral Peak, flowed hither, welded into one, and worked together. After eroding this Tenaya Lake basin, and all the splendidly sculptured rocks and mountains that surround and adorn it, and the great Tenaya Canyon, with its wealth of all that makes mountains sublime, they were welded with the vast South, Lyell, and Illilouette glaciers on one side, and with those of Hoffman on the other—thus forming a portion of a yet grander mer de glace in Yosemite Valley.

I reached the Tenaya Canyon, on my way home, by coming in from the northeast, rambling down over the shoulders of Mt. Watkins, touching bottom a mile above Mirror Lake. From thence home was but a saunter in the moonlight.

After resting one day, and the weather continuing calm, I ran up over the left shoulder of South Dome [Half Dome] and down in front of its grand split face to make some measurements, completed my work, climbed to the right shoulder, struck off along the ridge for Cloud's Rest, and reached the topmost heave of her sunny wave in ample time to see the sunset.

Cloud's Rest is a thousand feet higher than Tissiack [Half Dome]. It is a wavelike crest upon a ridge, which begins at Yosemite with Tissiack and runs continuously eastward to the thicket of peaks and crests around Lake Tenaya. This lofty granite wall is bent this way and that by the restless and weariless action of glaciers just as if it had been made of dough. But the grand circumference of mountains and forests are coming from far and near, densing into one close assemblage; for the sun, their god and father, with love ineffable, is glowing a sunset farewell. Not one of all the assembled rocks or trees seemed remote. How impressively their faces shone with responsive love!

I ran home in the moonlight with firm strides; for the sun-love made me strong. Down through the junipers; down through the firs; now in jet shadows, now in white light; over sandy moraines and bare, clanking rocks; past the huge ghost of South Dome rising weird through the firs; past the glorious fall of Nevada, the groves of Illilouette; through the pines of the valley; beneath the bright crystal sky blazing with stars. All of this mountain wealth in one day!—one of the rich ripe days that enlarge one's life; so much of the sun upon one side of it, so much of the moon and stars on the other.

8

A Near View of the High Sierra

In October 1872, Muir was returning to Yosemite Valley after exploring glaciers when he realized that it would be several months before he could return to his beloved high country. He decided on an impulse to climb the 11,500 foot Mt. Ritter, a rocky, barren peak in the Central Sierras. He climbed alone and without a coat, though winter was approaching.

This excerpt is from a chapter in The Mountains of California, *expanded from his journal account of the often quoted out-of-body episode he experienced at a perilous moment and which appears to have saved his life.*[75]

It was now about the middle of October, the springtime of snow-flowers. The first winter-clouds had already bloomed, and the peaks were strewn with fresh crystals, without, however, affecting the climbing to any dangerous extent. And as the weather was still profoundly calm and the distance to the foot of the mountain only a little more than a day, I felt that I was running no great risk of being storm-bound.

Mt. Ritter is king of the mountains of the middle portion of the High Sierra, as Shasta of the north and Whitney of the south sections. Moreover, as far as I know, it had never been climbed. I had explored the adjacent wilderness summer after summer, but my studies thus far had never drawn me to the top of it. Its height above sea-level is about 13,300 feet, and it is fenced round by steeply inclined glaciers and canyons of tremendous depth and ruggedness, which render it almost inaccessible. But difficulties of this kind only exhilarate the mountaineer.

My general plan was simply this: to scale the canyon wall, cross over to the eastern flank of the range, and then make my way southward to the northern spurs of Mt. Ritter in compliance with the intervening topography; for to push on directly southward from camp through the innumerable peaks and pinnacles that adorn this portion of the axis of the range, however interesting, would take too much time, besides being extremely difficult and dangerous at this time of year.

All my first day was pure pleasure; simply mountaineering indulgence, crossing the dry pathways of the ancient glaciers, tracing happy streams, and learning the habits of the birds and marmots in the groves and rocks. Before I had gone a mile from camp, I came to the foot of a white cascade that beats its way down a rugged gorge in the canyon wall, from a height of about nine hundred feet, and pours its throbbing waters into the Tuolumne. I was acquainted with its fountains, which, fortunately, lay in my course. What a fine traveling companion it proved to be, what songs it sang, and how passionately it told the mountain's own joy! Gladly I climbed along its dashing border, absorbing its divine music, and bathing from time to time in waftings of irised spray. Climbing higher, higher, new beauty came streaming on the sight: painted meadows, late-blooming gardens, peaks of rare architecture, lakes here and there, shining like silver, and glimpses of the forested middle region and the yellow lowlands far in the west. . . .

Passing a little way down over the summit until I had reached an elevation of about 10,000 feet, I pushed on southward toward a group of savage peaks that stand guard about Ritter on the north and west, groping my way, and dealing instinctively with every obstacle as it presented itself. Here a huge gorge would be found cutting across my path, along the dizzy edge of which

I scrambled until some less precipitous point was discovered where I might safely venture to the bottom and then, selecting some feasible portion of the opposite wall, reascend with the same slow caution. . . .

All the streams, too, and the pools at this elevation are furnished with little gardens wherever soil can be made to lie, which, though making scarce any show at a distance, constitute charming surprises to the appreciative observer. In these bits of leafiness a few birds find grateful homes. Having no acquaintance with man, they fear no ill, and flock curiously about the stranger, almost allowing themselves to be taken in the hand. In so wild and so beautiful a region was spent my first day, every sight and sound inspiring, leading one far out of himself, yet feeding and building up his individuality.

Now came the solemn, silent evening. Long, blue, spiky shadows crept out across the snow-fields, while a rosy glow, at first scarce discernible, gradually deepened and suffused every mountain-top, flushing the glaciers and the harsh crags above them. This was the alpenglow, to me one of the most impressive of all the terrestrial manifestations of God. At the touch of this divine light, the mountains seemed to kindle to a rapt, religious consciousness and stood hushed and waiting like devout worshipers. Just before the alpenglow began to fade, two crimson clouds came streaming across the summit like wings of flame, rendering the sublime scene yet more impressive; then came darkness and the stars. . . .

Icy Ritter was still miles away, but I could proceed no farther that night. I found a good camp ground on the rim of a glacier basin about 11,000 feet above the sea. A small lake nestles in the bottom of it, from which I got water for my tea, and a storm-beaten thicket nearby furnished abundance of resiny firewood. Somber peaks, hacked and shattered, circled half-way around the horizon, wearing a savage aspect in the gloaming, and a waterfall chanted solemnly across the lake on its way down from the foot of a glacier. The fall and the lake and the glacier were almost equally bare; while the scraggy pines anchored in the rock-fissures were so dwarfed and shorn by storm-winds that you might walk over their tops. In tone and aspect the scene was one of the most desolate I ever beheld. But the darkest scriptures of the mountains are illumined with bright passages of love that never fail to make themselves felt when one is alone.

I made my bed in a nook of the pine-thicket, where the branches were pressed and crinkled overhead like a roof and bent down around the sides. These are the best bedchambers the high mountains afford—snug as squirrel-nests, well ventilated, full of spicy odors, and with plenty of wind-played needles to sing one asleep. I little expected company, but, creeping in through a low side-door, I found five or six birds nestling among the tassels. The night-wind began to blow soon after dark; at first only a gentle breathing, but increasing toward midnight to a rough gale that fell upon my leafy roof in ragged surges like a cascade, bearing wild sounds from the crags overhead. The waterfall sang in chorus, filling the old ice-fountain with its solemn roar, and seeming to increase in power as the night advanced—fit voice for such a landscape. I had to creep out many times to the fire during the night, for it was biting cold and I had no blankets. Gladly I welcomed the morning star.

The dawn in the dry, wavering air of the desert was glorious. Everything encouraged my undertaking and betokened success. There was no cloud in the sky, no storm-tone in the wind. Breakfast of bread and tea was soon made. I fastened a hard, durable crust to my belt by way of provision, in case I should be compelled to pass a night on the mountain-top; then, securing the remainder of my little stock against wolves and wood-rats, I set forth free and hopeful.

How glorious a greeting the sun gives the mountains! To behold this alone is worth the pains of any excursion a thousand times over. The highest peaks burned like islands in a sea of liquid shade. Then the lower peaks and spires caught the glow, and long lances of light, streaming through many a notch and pass, fell thick on the frozen meadows. The majestic form of Ritter was full in sight, and I pushed rapidly on over rounded rock-bosses and pavements, my iron-shod shoes making a clanking sound, suddenly hushed now and then in rugs of bryanthus, and sedgy lake-margins soft as moss. . . .

All things were warming and awakening. Frozen rills began to flow, the marmots came out of their nests in boulder-piles and climbed sunny rocks to bask, and the dun-headed sparrows were flitting about seeking their breakfasts. The lakes seen from every ridge-top were brilliantly rippled and spangled, shimmering like the thickets of the low dwarf pines. The rocks, too, seemed responsive to the vital heat—rock-crystals and snow-crystals thrilling alike. I strode on exhilarated, as if never more to feel fatigue, limbs moving of themselves, every sense unfolding like the thawing flowers, to take part in the new day harmony.

All along my course thus far, excepting when down in the canyons, the landscapes were mostly open to me, and expansive, at least on one side. On the left were the purple plains of Mono, reposing dreamily and warm; on the right, the near peaks springing keenly into the thin sky with more and more impressive sublimity. But these larger views were at length lost. Rugged spurs, and moraines, and huge, projecting buttresses began to shut me in. Every feature became more rigidly alpine, without, however, producing any chilling effect; for going to the mountains is like going home. We always find that the strangest objects in these mountain wilds are in some degree familiar, and we look upon them with a vague sense of having seen them before.

Arriving on the summit of this dividing crest, one of the most exciting pieces of pure wilderness was disclosed that I ever discovered in all my mountaineering. There, immediately in front, loomed the majestic mass of Mt. Ritter, with a glacier swooping down its face nearly to my feet, then curving westward and pouring its frozen flood into a dark blue lake, whose shores were bound with precipices of crystalline snow; while a deep chasm drawn between the divide and the glacier separated the massive picture from everything else. I could see only the one sublime mountain, the one glacier, the one lake; the whole veiled with one blue shadow—rock, ice, and water close together without a single leaf or sign of life. After gazing spellbound, I began instinctively to scrutinize every notch and gorge and weathered buttress of the mountain, with reference to making the ascent. The entire front above the glacier appeared as one tremendous precipice, slightly receding at the top, and bristling with spires and pinnacles set above one another in formidable array. Massive lichen-stained battlements stood forward here and there, hacked at the top with angular notches, and separated by frosty gullies and recesses that have been veiled in shadow ever since their creation; while to right and left, as far as I could see, were huge, crumbling buttresses, offering no hope to the climber. The head of the glacier sends up a few finger-like branches through narrow *couloirs;* but these seemed too steep and short to be available, especially as I had no ax with which to cut steps, and the numerous narrow-throated gullies down which stones and snow are avalanched seemed hopelessly steep, besides being interrupted by vertical cliffs; while the whole front was rendered still more terribly forbidding by the chill shadow and the gloomy blackness of the rocks.

Descending the divide in a hesitating mood, I picked my way across the yawning chasm at the foot and climbed out upon the glacier. There were no meadows now to cheer with their brave colors, nor could I hear the dun-headed sparrows, whose cheery notes so often relieve the silence of our highest mountains. The only sounds were the gurgling of small rills down in the veins and crevasses of the glacier and now and then the rattling report of falling stones, with the echoes they shot out into the crisp air.

I could not distinctly hope to reach the summit from this side, yet I moved on across the glacier as if driven by fate. Contending with myself, the season is too far spent, I said, and even should I be successful, I might be storm-bound on the mountain; and in the cloud-darkness, with the cliffs and crevasses covered with snow, how could I escape? No; I must wait till next summer. I would only approach the mountain now, and inspect it, creep about its flanks, learn what I could of its history, holding myself ready to flee on the approach of the first storm-cloud. But we little know until tried how much of the uncontrollable there is in us, urging across glaciers and torrents, and up dangerous heights, let the judgment forbid as it may.

I succeeded in gaining the foot of the cliff on the eastern extremity of the glacier and there discovered the mouth of a narrow avalanche gully, through which I began to climb, intending to follow it as far as possible, and at least obtain some fine wild views for my pains. Its general course is oblique to the plane of the mountain-face, and the metamorphic slates of which the mountain is built are cut by cleavage planes in such a way that they weather off in angular blocks, giving rise to irregular steps that greatly facilitate climbing on the sheer places. I thus made my way into a wilderness of crumbling spires and battlements, built together in bewildering combinations, and glazed in many places with a thin coating of ice, which I had to hammer off with stones. The situation was becoming gradually more perilous; but, having passed several dangerous spots, I dared not think of descending; for, so steep was the entire ascent, one would inevitably fall to the glacier in case a single misstep were made. Knowing, therefore, the tried danger beneath, I became all the more anxious concerning the developments to be made above, and began to be conscious of a vague foreboding of what actually befell; not that I was given to fear, but rather because my instincts, usually so positive and true, seemed vitiated in some way, and were leading me astray.

At length, after attaining an elevation of about 12,800 feet, I found myself at the foot of a sheer drop in the bed of the avalanche channel I was tracing, which seemed absolutely to bar further progress. It was only about forty-five or fifty feet high, and somewhat roughened by fissures and projections; but these seemed so slight and insecure as footholds that I tried hard to avoid the precipice altogether by scaling the wall of the channel on either side. But, though less steep, the walls were smoother than the obstructing rock, and repeated efforts only showed that I must either go right ahead or turn back. The tried dangers beneath seemed even greater than that of the cliff in front; therefore, after scanning its face again and again, I began to scale it, picking my holds with intense caution. After gaining a point about halfway to the top, I was suddenly brought to a dead stop, with arms outspread, clinging close to the face of the rock, unable to move hand or foot either up or down. My doom appeared fixed. I *must* fall. There would be a moment of bewilderment, and then a lifeless rumble down the one general precipice to the glacier below.

When this final danger flashed upon me, I became nerve-shaken for the first time since setting foot on the mountains, and my mind seemed to fill with a stifling smoke. But this terrible eclipse lasted only a moment, when life blazed forth again with preternatural clearness. I seemed suddenly to become possessed of a new sense. The other self, bygone experiences, Instinct, or Guardian Angel—call it what you will—came forward and assumed control. Then my trembling muscles became firm again, every rift and flaw in the rock was seen as through a microscope, and my limbs moved with a positiveness and precision with which I seemed to have nothing at all to do. Had I been borne aloft upon wings, my deliverance could not have been more complete.

Above this memorable spot, the face of the mountain is still more savagely hacked and torn. It is a maze of yawning chasms and gullies, in the angles of which rise beetling crags and piles of detached boulders that seem to have been gotten ready to be launched below. But the strange influx of strength I had received seemed inexhaustible. I found a way without effort and soon stood upon the topmost crag in the blessed light.

How truly glorious the landscape circled around this noble summit!—giant mountains, valleys innumerable, glaciers and meadows, rivers and lakes, with the wide blue sky bent tenderly over them all. But in my first hour of freedom from that terrible shadow, the sunlight in which I was laving seemed all in all. . . .

The eye, rejoicing in its freedom, roves about the vast expanse, yet returns again and again to the mountain peaks. Perhaps some one of the multitude excites special attention, some gigantic castle with turret and battlement, or some Gothic cathedral more abundantly spired than Milan's. But, generally, when looking for the first time from an all-embracing standpoint like this, the inexperienced observer is oppressed by the incomprehensible grandeur, variety, and abundance of the mountains rising shoulder to shoulder beyond the reach of vision; and it is only after they have been studied one by one, long and lovingly, that their far-reaching harmonies become manifest. Then, penetrate the wilderness where you may, the main telling features, to which all the surrounding topography is subordinate, are quickly perceived, and the most complicated clusters of peaks stand revealed harmoniously correlated and fashioned like works of art—eloquent monuments of the ancient ice-rivers that brought them into relief from the general mass of the range. The canyons, too, some of them a mile deep, mazing wildly through the mighty host of mountains, however lawless and ungovernable at first sight they appear, are at length recognized as the necessary effects of causes which followed each other in harmonious sequence—Nature's poems carved on tables of stone—the simplest and most emphatic of her glacial compositions. . . .

But in the midst of these fine lessons and landscapes, I had to remember that the sun was wheeling far to the west, while a new way down the mountain had to be discovered to some point on the timber line where I could have a fire; for I had not even burdened myself with a coat. I first scanned the western spurs, hoping some way might appear through which I might reach the northern glacier, and cross its snout; or pass around the lake into which it flows, and thus strike my morning track. This route was soon sufficiently unfolded to show that, if practicable at all, it would require so much time that reaching camp that night would be out of the question. I therefore scrambled back eastward, descending the southern slopes obliquely at the same time. Here the crags seemed less formidable, and the head of a glacier that flows northeast came in sight, which I determined to follow as far as possible, hoping thus to make my way to the foot of the peak on the east side and thence across the intervening canyons and ridges to camp. . . .

Night drew near before I reached the eastern base of the mountain, and my camp lay many a rugged mile to the north; but ultimate success was assured. It was now only a matter of endurance and ordinary mountain-craft. The sunset was, if possible, yet more beautiful than that of the day before. The Mono landscape seemed to be fairly saturated with warm, purple light. The peaks marshaled along the summit were in shadow, but through every notch and pass streamed vivid sunfire, soothing and irradiating their rough, black angles, while companies of small, luminous clouds hovered above them like very angels of light.

Darkness came on, but I found my way by the trends of the canyons and the peaks projected against the sky. All excitement died with the light, and then I was weary. But the joyful sound of the waterfall across the lake was heard at last, and soon the stars were seen reflected in the lake itself. Taking my bearings from these, I discovered the little pine thicket in which my nest was, and then I had a rest such as only a tired mountaineer may enjoy. After lying loose and lost for awhile, I made a sunrise fire, went down to the lake, dashed water on my head, and dipped a cupful for tea. The revival brought about by bread and tea was as complete as the exhaustion from excessive enjoyment and toil. Then I crept beneath the pine-tassels to bed. The wind was frosty and the fire burned low, but my sleep was none the less sound, and the evening constellations had swept far to the west before I awoke.   —MC, 37–45

Notes

1. JOM, 118.
2. KRS, 114.
3. LL, 1:xx.
4. JOM, 86.
5. JOM, xii.
6. Two of his most spiritually intimate pieces to see publication at the time of their writing, the Calypso letter (April 1864) and "A Geologist's Winter Walk" (February 1871), were published by the recipients without Muir's knowledge.
7. Michael Cohen, *The Pathless Way: John Muir and American Wilderness* (Madison: University of Wisconsin Press, 1984) places Muir in the tradition of Zen Buddhist mystics. Frederick Turner (*John Muir, Rediscovering America* [Cambridge, Mass.: Perseus Publishing, 1985]) compares Muir's spiritual experiences in Yosemite to classical descriptions of religious conversions. Thurman Wilkins (*John Muir, Apostle of Nature* [Norman: University of Oklahoma Press, 1995]) views Muir as a mystical pantheist. Charles Pelfrey ("Elements of Mysticism in the Writings of John Burroughs and John Muir," Ph.D. dissertation, University Microfilms International, 1958) places Muir's experience within Evelyn Underhill's classic stages of mystical development. Donald Wurster's biography (*A Passion for Nature: The Life of John Muir* [New York: Oxford University Press, 2008]) suggests that Muir's spiritual sources are best located in a modified form of transcendentalism.
8. SBY, 223.
9. KRS, 80.

10. SBY, 287.

11. Bonnie Gisel, *Nature's Beloved Son: Rediscovering John Muir's Botanical Legacy* (Berkeley, Calif.: Heyday Books, 2008), 43-44.

12. KRS, 29.

13. Turner, *John Muir*, 122–23.

14. Gretel Erlich, *John Muir, Nature's Visionary* (Washington, D.C.: National Geographic, 2000), 54.

15. KRS, 57.

16. Muir would visit the family thirty years later after he had become famous.

17. KRS, 71–74.

18. Thurman Wilkins, *John Muir: Apostle of Nature* (Norman: University of Oklahoma Press, 1995), 60.

19. JOM, 69.

20. L. M. Wolfe, *Son of the Wilderness: The Life of John Muir* (New York: Knopf, 1945; reprint ed., Madison: University of Wisconsin Press, 1978), 144. Muir's friend, the artist William Keith, said Muir's close circle "almost thought he was Jesus Christ." Keith nicknamed Muir "the prophet Jeremiah." See Wolfe, 154.

21. Ibid., 144.

22. KRS, 151.

23. KRS, 146.

24. Muir: "It seems strange that visitors to Yosemite should be so little influenced by its novel grandeur, as if their eyes were bandaged and their ears stopped. Most of those I saw yesterday were looking down as if wholly unconscious of anything going on about them, while the sublime rocks were trembling with the tones of the mighty chanting congregation of waters gathered from all the mountains roundabout, making music that might draw Angels out of heaven. " MFS, 255–56.

25. JOM, xiii.

26. KRS, 147.

27. KRS, 249.

28. JOM, 282.

29. Huston Smith, *Forgotten Truth: The Common Vision of the World's Religions* (San Francisco: HarperSanFrancisco, 1976), 113.

30. "The Treasures of the Yosemite," and "Features of the Proposed Yosemite National Park," appeared in the August and September 1889 issues of the *Century*.

31. ONP, 1.

32. Donald Worster, *A Passion for Nature: The Life of John Muir* (New York: Oxford University Press), 329.

33. Wolfe, *Son of the Wilderness*, 268.

34. DP, 48.

35. Dayton Duncan, *The National Parks: America's Best Idea:* An illustrated history with a preface by Ken Burns (New York: Alfred A. Knopf, 2009), 94.

36. DP, 83.

37. KRS, 248.

38. MFS, 103.

39. JOM, 80–82.

40. JOM, 92.

41. MFS, 319.

42. LL, 1:332–33.

43. TMW, 98-99.

44. JOM, 277–78.

45. JOM, 137–38.

46. LL, 2:215–16.

47. JOM, 137–38.

48. MFS, 324–27.

49. JOM, 440.

50. This is the first of Muir's writings to be published. James Butler took Muir's letter from a table at Carr's house and, without telling her or Muir, sent it to the *Boston Recorder* for publication. One of Muir's strongest supporters, Butler described the

twenty-seven-year-old wanderer as an "inspired pilgrim . . . not a whit behind Thoreau as a scrutinizer and votary of nature," and gifted with "esoteric raptures in his close communion with the virgin nature." Muir's account, presented here, was written forty-five years after the episode occurred, and it is possible he had forgotten the actual circumstances of its publication. See KRS, 23. See also William Kimes and Maymie Kimes, *John Muir: A Reading Bibliography* (Fresno, Calif.: Panorama West Books, 1986), 1.

51. Michael P. Cohen, *The Pathless Way: John Muir and American Wilderness* (Madison: University of Wisconsin Press, 1984), 8.

52. Turner, *John Muir,* 122–23.

53. LL, 1:xx.

54. The passage combines versions from Turner, *John Muir, Rediscovering America,* 132, and LL, 1:158.

55. Turner, *John Muir,* 166.

56. KRS, 83.

57. R. Engberg and D. Wesling, eds., *John Muir: To Yosemite and Beyond* (Salt Lake City: University of Utah Press, 1999), 51–52. This is excerpted from an unrevised version of the passage published in *My First Summer in the Sierras* for June 6, 1869.

58. Muir's experience echoes that of the America Quaker visionary John Woolman, who hears a voice in a dream proclaiming, "John Woolman is dead." Woolman was transformed by the experience.

59. Elizabeth I. Dixon, ed., "Some New John Muir Letters," *Southern California Quarterly* 46, no. 3 (September 1964): 249–50, in Engberg and Wesling, *John Muir,* 63–65.

60. Wolfe, *Son of the Wilderness,* 144.

61. John Muir (March 26, 2012) in Stephen K. Hatch, *The Contemplative John Muir: Spiritual Quotations from the Great American Naturalist,* 76. Kindle edition.